Ethnic Jewelry

Ethnic Jewelry

edited by
John Mack

Harry N. Abrams, Inc.,
Publishers, New York

Library of Congress Cataloging in Publication Data

Ethnic Jewelry.

Bibliography: p.
Includes index.
1. Ethnic jewelry.   I. Mack, John.
NK4890.E8684 1988   739.27   88-3333
ISBN 0-8109-3

Published by Harry N. Abrams, Incorporated, New York

A Times Mirror Company

Printed and bound in Italy

Half title page Silver gilded breast ornament
inlaid with cornelians; Türkmen (see 43)

Title page Mongolian gold head-dress set with
turquoises and coloured stones (see 152)

This page Silver pin or *tapu* from Andean Chile (see p. 153)

Contents

Preface

♦

Deciding on the title of a book is always
a potentially hazardous business. In this case *Ethnic Jewellery* seemed the closest to a
succinct and readily comprehensible description of the kinds of topic to be covered. It
does, however, require a little further explanation.

Firstly, it will be plain from the character of what follows that we have not treated either
word in any over-precise sense. As the opening chapter is intended to demonstrate,
definitions of where jewellery stops and apparently different forms of decoration take
over are far from clear. Indeed, it is argued that the full understanding of the range of
significance of individual pieces of 'jewellery' takes us into a much wider field of study.
We might, for instance, be obliged to take account of other techniques of bodily
adornment (of which wearing particular objects may be only part), movement and
gesture (which affect how they are seen), the symbolism of materials, patterns of
inheritance, and the social and ritual context within which such items are displayed.
Some of these points are taken up by other authors in subsequent chapters.

Similarly, it should be mentioned at the outset that what seems at first sight to be
indisputably *jewellery* may in many societies serve purposes beyond those of mere
decoration. We have not, for instance, sought to draw any hard and fast lines between
jewellery and amulets, though in common understanding the one serves largely decorative functions and the other possesses essentially magical properties. For present
purposes both have seemed to us relevant to discuss, particularly when it is realised that
those who make and use such items of adornment may themselves not distinguish
between them in such terms.

The word 'ethnic' is beset by similar problems if interpreted too precisely. Again, it is
difficult to be clear where to stop and start. What is intended here is an emphasis on the
forms and techniques of jewellery manufacture that characterise the non-European
world. This is not to say that, had space allowed, a consideration of European folk
jewellery would not have been relevant, and clearly many of the technological and, for
that matter, anthropological processes described in what follows could equally be said to
typify certain regions of Europe or America and particular periods in the history of
Western culture. Equally we have taken the occasion of this publication to include a

review of the jewellery of Precolumbian America. This is not because it is felt that any essential or necessary continuity needs to be asserted between the pre- and post-Conquest traditions of the New World to make them comprehensible – as will appear, there are in fact significant breaks in the history of Latin American jewellery manufacture which largely coincide with the period of Spanish exploitation of America. None the less, from a technical (no less than from an aesthetic) point of view we thought it important to include a section documenting the rich traditions of parts of the Americas to give a fuller sense of historical perspective to the subject in a region where the evidence is especially full.

The objects that have been selected to illustrate the book are from a variety of sources. The majority, however, are drawn from the British Museum's extensive collections, and in particular those held by the Department of Ethnography at the Museum of Mankind. Yet the book has not been conceived in any sense as a guide to these collections and the subjects covered do not necessarily reflect in any exclusive way their strengths and weaknesses. The contributing authors have instead been invited to reflect in their various chapters on the types of materials, technological features, and to a degree, the themes that characterise the regions of which they have a specialist knowledge. To that extent the intention has been to gather together materials that might serve as an introduction to the subject as a whole rather than to try and catalogue or record the particularities of any individual collection. A detailed bibliography has been included to increase the general usefulness of this volume.

We begin, then, with a review of some of the main features that emerge in the anthropological literature on jewellery. This chapter focuses on the enlarged sense which the term may be required to possess in non-European contexts. The core of the book is the set of regional surveys which seek to give comprehensive coverage of jewellery-making traditions around the world. Finally, we conclude with a more detailed discussion of the technological processes involved in the manufacture of jewellery. This has the incidental virtue of avoiding undue repetition in the body of the book when essentially similar techniques may be employed in diverse regions and indeed on different continents. It also, however, enables us to see why with comparable technologies apparently similar effects may sometimes come to characterise the jewellery of quite unrelated peoples.

Assembling all the material and assuring a consistency amongst it has been a demanding editorial task. Acknowledgement is more than due to the unstinting efforts of Jenny Chattington of British Museum Publications, who went through the chapters thoroughly as they were prepared and has helped immeasurably in giving shape and unity to the book as a whole. Credits for illustrations selected for inclusion are given separately. We should, however, mention that those photographs of items in the collections of the British Museum and the Horniman Museum were taken by the British Museum's Photographic Service. We would like in particular to thank Ivor Kerslake, Kate Warren and David Agar for their patience and their efforts.

Introduction

♦

ADORNING THE BODY, EXPRESSING THE PERSON

Often in my atrabiliar-moods, when I read of pompous ceremonials, Frankfort Coronations, Royal Drawing-rooms, Levees, Couchees . . . and I strive in my remote privacy, to form a clear picture of that solemnity, – on a sudden, as by some enchanter's wand, the – shall I speak it? – the Clothes fly-off the whole dramatic corps; and Dukes, Grandees, Bishops, Generals. Anointed Presence itself, every mother's son of them; stand straddling there, not a shirt on them; and I know not whether to laugh or weep.

CARLYLE, *Sartor Resartus*, p. 45

1 Bella woman from Burkina Faso wearing a variety of beaded and other ornaments. Coins are a common form of hair decoration across this part of the southern Sahara (whether French francs or Maria Theresa dollars are used). Melted down, such coinage is an important source of silver from which other forms of jewellery are fashioned.

Thomas Carlyle, the nineteenth-century historian and social commentator, had his invented Professor of Things in General, Herr Diogenes Teufelsdrockh, imagine the unimaginable; in *Sartor Resartus* Professor Teufelsdrockh, a 'speculative radical', reflects on the character of a society that is *not* founded upon clothes and personal adornment. Kings wrestle naked with coach drivers. Both have the same viscera, tissues, livers and other 'life-tackle'; indeed, the coach driver with his practical intelligence is as like as not the more gifted of the two. Yet in reality the social gulf between them is immense. Professor Teufelsdrockh is not slow to identify the source of their inequality – 'from clothes', he says unhesitatingly (p. 47).

This might seem a somewhat eccentric sketch against which to set an introduction to the subject of ethnic jewellery. One of its themes – the use of different types and styles of decoration to indicate distinctions of rank and status – is certainly common to all discussions of forms of personal adornment: jewellery merges into regalia. But Carlyle, of course, is not talking merely literally. His purpose is to discuss in this oblique way the social and moral climate of his times, and, more basically, to reveal something of the human condition in general. Thus he draws a consistent distinction between inner spiritual states and the visible wrappings in which such conditions are clad. Clothes to that extent are not simply woven vestments – they are also a metaphor for the various elements of which the social world is constructed, a metaphor for language, ritual, art, beliefs and ideas.

Jewellery, too, can be examined in a somewhat similar light. Not only anthropologists

9

2 One of a pair of women's brass anklets, Igbo, Nigeria. Though cumbersome and heavy, such prestigious objects were often worn into middle age. This example is 13 inches in diameter, and its surface is decorated with punched designs.

evaluate personal adornment as a reflection of states of mind or being but their informants also often appear to discuss and assess styles of decoration after the manner of Carlyle and his fictitious authority Teufelsdrockh. Ornamenting the body, as will emerge, may often express a whole range of personal and social conditions and not simply embellish physical appearances.

Jewellery, of course, is only one part of body decoration. To that extent it is at once a precise and yet a limiting point of departure. Styles of clothing, body-painting, tattooing, scarification, the filing or extraction of teeth, and circumcision are equally important. Most involve actual physical alteration of the body and to that extent create a more permanent and dramatic transformation than does the wearing of jewellery. Movements, gestures and general deportment are also relevant. Indeed, these may be so characteristic that they may be reproduced so as to suggest the presence of adornment even when it is not in fact being worn. Igbo women in Nigeria, for instance, typically wear heavy brass anklets of plate-like proportions which cause them to have a rolling gait as they walk. This style of movement is often imitated by those who are not adorned in this way to suggest that they too are accustomed to decorating in such a prestigious manner. In the available literature it is these broader aspects, rather than jewellery as an isolated topic of interest, that have tended to be the main focus of attention.

Jewellery is also set apart from other means of transforming physical appearance in that it appears familiar: we think we know what it is and what it does. However, although the physical alteration of the body may be regarded as an act of beautification by those who practise it, it is often characterised by others as barbaric and brutish. An instructive illustration is provided by the Sara of Chad in Africa. Amongst these peoples it is the tradition for women to make an incision in the lower lip into which a small wood disc is inserted. Gradually the size of this disc is increased until mature women are able to support large lip-plates that extend the lower part of their mouths. The Sara offer two alternative versions for the origin of this practice. One is that it enhances female attractiveness according to local ideas; the other notes that since outsiders find such styles of decoration ugly it was a good way of protecting women against the threat of being taken as slaves, a real possibility in the past. Mutilation, then, is the opposite side of the same coin as beautification, a factor on which both the Sara and for that matter the contemporary punk fashions of the Western world mount their own particular commentary.

Interestingly, too, both lip-plates and elements of punk decoration would seem to fall within the same general realm of adornment as necklaces, bracelets, pendants, and especially ear-rings – yet they appear to sit uneasily in such company. Jewellery is conventionally seen in the West as something attractive in itself, capable of lending character and elegance to the wearer. However, the lip-plate, separated from the lip, is frequently unadorned and unexceptional. It is also made of a mundane material: wood. Jewellery, by contrast, is more readily associated in Western thought with durable and often with rare materials; on that account it is characteristically expensive, an apt candidate to be passed on as a family heirloom and to be mentioned specifically in both insurance policies and wills.

In a way the lip-plate is, of course, an extreme example within the field of what is

3 Pendant from the Solomon Islands. It is composed of a wide range of materials: the central ring is shell within which has been mounted carved turtleshell; the surround comprises beads, small teeth and buttons.

4 *Left* Necklace from the Bedouin of the Negev Desert. The materials used include beads of various sorts, coral, mother-of-pearl, cotton tassels, a shirt button for the fastening, and cloves, whose pleasant scent adds another dimension.

termed ethnic jewellery. Most items of adornment from distant places can be as comfortably accommodated on European or American bodies as they can on African, Indian or New Guinean ones. They can also be made of many more dazzling materials than wood: of gold and silver, gemstones, ivory, shell, coral and beads amongst many others. The temptation for Westerners is to think that all jewellery is essentially doing the same thing – rendering ornate, beautifying, and little else besides. A few examples will help establish a much broader function than this and will introduce some of the themes that will emerge in other parts of this book.

In Madagascar a whole range of ornaments was commonly worn by higher-ranking members of the Merina kingdom, particularly in the nineteenth century. Silver was especially favoured, and its use dates back at least to the early part of that century. The silver was derived from imported coins, for the most part Maria Theresa dollars. Melted down, such silver coins could be beaten into thin rods and drawn to make wire. This was then made into chains to which coins themselves were sometimes attached. Images such as that of the humped cattle of Madagascar, small hatchets and silver needles would also be strung on wire. Finger- and ear-rings, headbands and bracelets were frequently made of silver. Finally, a beaded box with silver 'teeth' projecting from the bottom was worn round the waist. This, during the nineteenth century, developed into a much more ornate object, the beads replaced by coloured imitations of precious stones and the 'teeth' sometimes rendered in gold. The teeth represented those of crocodiles, the only serious predators on the island of Madagascar and an appropriate metaphor of power.

At one level such jewellery appears to share many qualities with its Euro-American counterparts. It is made of precious materials; it is taken out for special occasions (particularly, in Imerina, for display at circumcision ceremonies); and it could be passed on down the generations as an enduring heirloom. It represented an inheritance of the wealthy – in fact, certain heavier silver chains were acquired only after a dignitary had already bought enough slaves to sustain his household. Yet the fact that such items are made of silver had an additional significance, for silver is 'attractive' in several senses. Silver in Malagasy (the language of Madagascar) is *volafotsy*, 'white money'. As its use in

5 *Right* Bejewelled gold box from Madagascar, with a silk brocaded sash which enables it to be worn across the chest. The prongs at the bottom are intended to recall crocodiles' teeth, which are deemed to have protective qualities. This example is said to date from about 1820.

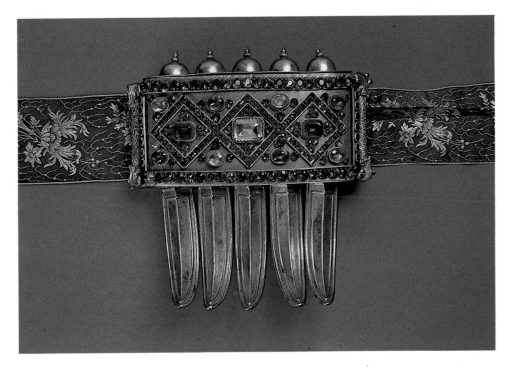

other contexts makes clear, white is a colour associated with attracting ancestral blessings. White shawls, for example, are worn by those in mourning not so much as a colour of grief – and thus equivalent to the black clothing worn virtually everywhere else – but as a means of associating oneself with the source of blessings when in the uncertain mystical state of bereavement. Silver coins were given to the monarch at certain times of the year in return for the blessings of royalty; and coins continue to be tossed into a medical preparation whilst the ancestors are invoked as a means of rendering it effective. Silver jewellery was not simply a thing of beauty and a token of wealth; it was also a superior form of charm, a means simultaneously of attracting the attention of the living and the blessings of the ancestors.

The islands that make up the modern nation-state of Indonesia provide an equally instructive example of the additional significance apparently familiar forms of jewellery may possess in their local context. Here it was not silver coinage but gold that was the relevant import. Small-time aristocrats in a number of places traded livestock and labour to gain access to the gold coinage from which local craftsmen might fashion ostentatious metal versions of the traditional feather and shell ornaments of noble families. Crowns, regalia, breast-plates and amulets were all manufactured and came to express the mystical and physical power of aristocratic families. Such jewellery, however, was not conceived as aesthetic adornment so much as a means of honouring the ancestors and securing a continued flow of ancestral protection. It declared simultaneously a worldly importance and a privileged relationship with the ancestral spirits.

It was not even essential that it should be worn by nobility themselves for the point to be made. Thus on the Indonesian islands of Sumba and Flores gold ornaments, technically owned by royalty, were not in fact donned by their proprietors, but employed rather by those entering potentially dangerous states of trance on their behalf. At the funerals of noblemen, for example, Sumba slaves would be bedecked in an extravagant display of gold pendants, beaten gold crescentic ornaments and quantities of heavy gold chain. Although provided from noble resources, such elaborate finery threatened to outdo the ornamentation of aristocrats. Thus adorned, the slaves could fall into trance

6 Torajan man from Sulawesi, Indonesia, who bears the title *induk aluk*, literally 'mother of tradition'. His ornamentation is exclusive to persons of such elevated rank and includes a necklace of wood tubes covered with gold and another of boars' tusks carved to look like crocodile teeth.

7 'Necklace' from the Andaman Islands composed of fibre wrapped round human bone. It is said to have protective and curative qualities. Thus someone afflicted with toothache would wear it round the face.

and establish relations between the living assembly, the deceased noblemen and the community of the ancestors. Jewellery here continues to set people apart; but in this case it is slaves and those entranced, people beyond the margins of ordinary society, who are thereby marked out.

Such reference in adornment to external and potent mystical forces is not uncommon. In the Andaman Islands adults traditionally wear a necklace of human bones. These bones are regarded as the repository of beneficial powers that derive from the dead. Thus, when worn as reliquaries, they become powerful magical devices, a defence against the influence of evil forces. The point this makes is one familiar to ethnographers: that the significance attaching to apparently comparable phenomena, whether objects such as items of jewellery, events or social institutions, frequently shifts according to local cultural idioms and circumstances. The issue is clearest where objects are traded; frequently they take on a totally different set of associations amongst those acquiring them from those they hold for the trader. Thus it is possible nowadays to acquire necklaces of bone, tree-roots and beads from fashionable shops in Europe or America. In this setting it has ceased to be of major significance that the bones might originally have been used in Africa in divination and the roots ground up to make medicines. In its shop window or on the neck of a purchaser it is palpably exotic. Like a deep sun-tan in mid-winter it has come to be suggestive of an interesting and alluring way of life. The necklace, however, may have been created simply as a convenient means for a traditional healer to transport the tools of his trade. And in that context, arguably, it was not jewellery at all; when purchased in Liberty's of London, on the other hand, it unquestionably has become so.

The reverse of this situation, it might be noted, also occurs. The sight of people

15

8 Gold spectacles which lack the lenses and have instead a mesh of gold wire. Such decorative jewellery has attained considerable popularity in recent years in parts of West Africa, and is the speciality of the Baule of the Ivory Coast, amongst whom this example was collected.

carrying large bundles of keys is a familiar enough one in many parts of the world. This need not, however, necessarily entail ownership of innumerable locked-up possessions. It is enough that the keys should imply access to the products of industrialised countries, and thus a certain importance on the part of the wearer, for them to act perfectly well as adornment. Similarly, gold spectacles have recently became a fashionable adornment in the Ivory Coast and elsewhere in West Africa. Here the lenses are replaced by thin gold wire meshes which act not to aid vision, but if anything to impede it. Such fancy spectacles have clearly become jewellery in a similar way to the diviner's bones and medicines. Both, extracted from their usual context, re-emerge as beguiling decoration.

Many other illustrations in this book from diverse parts of the globe might be given as examples of the process. Here it is only necessary to point to a number of preliminary instances. Thus amongst the Mapuche Indians of Chile, for instance, a kind of link chain often with coins and pendants attached is a typical component of female costume. It may be worn round the forehead as a kind of wreath, or it may be attached beneath the shoulders so that it hangs down over the breasts. When acquired, however, by the Guachos and the Huasos (respectively the Argentinian and Chilean versions of cowboys) these same chains are recycled as ornate horse tackle, as holders for spurs or as reins and halters.

Coins are the most susceptible to this kind of treatment, as the examples from Madagascar and Indonesia have already suggested. To act as currency, a medium of exchange, is often the least of the functions performed by coinage. Thus, in similar vein, Spanish and Mexican coins were once much in demand in Egypt on account of the amuletic qualities attributed to their characteristic pillar designs. Sudan had equivalent traditions, and there are even reports of a metalworker in Shendy who succeeded in making his living by altering the legends on Spanish pillar dollars. In the latter part of the nineteenth century French coinage, too, became popular in Sudan, and Sudanese silversmiths became adept at reproducing their own versions of coins for use as pendants. One stereotyped image that became characteristic showed three figures standing side by side. It was copied from the heavy French five-franc piece of the Third Republic which showed on the reverse side three figures beneath the tripartite motto of the 1789 Revolution, *Liberté, Egalité, Fraternité*.

The process of creating jewellery, then, often involves manipulating the context within which an object appears. And it does not have to be of exotic origin for this to be possible.

9 Riang woman from Tripura, India, bedecked with silver jewellery including rigid armlets and cuffs, as well as necklaces and rings ornamented with quantities of coins. The coins are old Indian silver rupees dating from the British colonial period, and are a highly valued symbol of wealth.

Functional objects from within a culture can be recycled so as to serve significant decorative purposes. Tibetan Buddhists, for instance, turn the handles of prayer wheels as an accompaniment to devotions. Installed between the cylinder and handle are washers which are usually made of conch shells. As these wear out they are often strung together as necklaces, witness to the zealous piety of the wearer whose attention to religious devotions rendered them inoperative in their original context.

Just as the significance of individual items of jewellery may differ from place to place, so too notions of which parts of the body it might be appropriate to decorate are variable. This is perhaps particularly obvious in those cases where the body itself has had to be transformed in some way to accommodate the ornamentation. Ear-lobes, for instance, may not only be pierced but also extended to allow plugs to be inserted, as amongst the Maasai of Kenya; lips may be incised, and extended as we have seen; and shoulders may be artificially lowered by wearing a gradually increasing number of brass rings round the 10 neck, as amongst Padaung women of Burma. Quite apart from the more obvious significance of shape, colour and materials, how and where ornament is worn matter.

For example, among the Suya Indians of central Brazil both men and women wear 11 large discs in their ears. These are made of wood or rolled palm leaf and are painted with white clay. Men (and not women, as is usually the case in Africa) also have large wooden discs inserted in the lower lip and painted bright red on the top and sides. By contrast with this emphasis on ear and mouth, neither the eyes nor the nose is generally decorated by either sex.

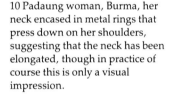

10 Padaung woman, Burma, her neck encased in metal rings that press down on her shoulders, suggesting that the neck has been elongated, though in practice of course this is only a visual impression.

This in its turn can be related to the complex of ideas which are associated with hearing (and thus the ears) and with speaking (and the mouth). For the Suya the phrase 'I hear' bears much the same meaning as the English 'I see'. To hear is also to understand, to gain knowledge. By extension it also acquires a moral quality – it describes a person who follows social codes and rules. The ear, therefore, is associated with the virtues of intelligent 'insight' (as we would say) and conformity. Indeed, something well learnt and committed to memory is said to be 'in the ear'. It is thus appropriately emphasised in the characteristic decoration adopted by both sexes.

Speech has a similar central role in Suya life and explains the attention given to the mouth in decoration. An emphasis on vision and a keen sense of smell are by contrast associated with witches in the one case and animals or anti-social phenomena in the other. The eyes and the nose are thus left undecorated other than in very exceptional circumstances, whilst the ear and mouth are emphasised by being both decorated and physically enlarged. The white colour of the ear-disc is associated with coolness and receptivity, the red of the lip-plate with fiery oratory.

Does this mean, therefore, that where a particular part of the body is emphasised in adornment it can be assumed it is also something of a local cultural obsession? It is, for instance, usual to interpret a profusion of linguistic terms around a particular topic in this way. Certainly, as far as lip-plugs are concerned, another example, that of the Fali in northern Cameroon, broadly confirms Suya practice in Brazil. Among the Fali it is women who wear lip-plugs, which, it is said, make them look like frogs. This refers to the

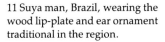

11 Suya man, Brazil, wearing the wood lip-plate and ear ornament traditional in the region.

ancestral woman of the Fali who was taught the things of women by a frog. Women are responsible for passing on this ancestral wisdom to their daughters, and the impact of their instruction is enhanced both by attention to the mouth, the source of speech, through personal decoration, and by the more remote allusion to the frog, the original source of the teaching itself.

Many societies also give particular attention to the nose. Even if it is not ornamented in some way it may be physically altered, broken and flattened as in Polynesia, or straightened and shortened as in Europe. In Papua New Guinea the septum and the alae are often pierced to accommodate varieties of shell, plumage, and boars' tusks. There are, no doubt, variations in how exactly the nose is regarded over such a wide area as the vast island of New Guinea. With such elaborate traditions of personal decoration as are found there any single explanation is unlikely to cover all possibilities. Amongst the Wahgi at least, however, it seems that it is not any particular connection of the nose with the faculty of smell that is the relevant association. On the model of Suya practice that might have seemed likely. The nose is rather regarded more comprehensively as the metaphorical seat for a wide range of emotions and to that extent may be taken to stand for the whole person.

The siting of jewellery can also act to divide the body into zones, in addition to any capacity it has for expanding the associations of particular organs. The neck, for instance, is often an area of special attention. The massing of jewellery round the neck effects a striking visual – and thus, arguably, conceptual – separation of the head from the body. This is especially notable amongst some of the pastoralist peoples of East Africa, peoples such as the Maasai, Samburu, Turkana or Karimajong. Here it is often the practice for women to adorn the neck with beads sometimes numbering up to sixty and more strings and cover the whole area from the chin down to and over the top of the shoulders. The head, too, is often ornamented in some way, and armlets are common. The effect of numerous colourful strings of beads massed in the area of the neck is, however, visually dominant.

The beads of which such strings are composed are imported and have long been extensively traded throughout Eastern Africa. To that extent, as with so many traditions, adornment is often said to represent an investment in movable wealth. For men their herds of cattle and goats represent the sum of their worldly standing; for women it is bead necklaces, which are not put on for particular events but worn more or less all the time by those entitled to decorate in that manner.

No doubt it could be argued that the neck is the only place on the body for such bead necklaces to be conveniently carried, and in such societies, following a semi-nomadic or transhumant life, portability is of crucial importance. Yet beyond this practical consideration it is notable that many related peoples in this region make some distinction between the head and the heart. As elsewhere, the head is seen as the seat of the intellect, the heart of the emotions and metaphorically associated with many other essentially moral conditions. Reference to the heart expresses intentions, states of doubt or uncertainty, fear, envy, contentment, and so forth. It is interesting therefore that it should be the neck, a neutral zone, which is often elaborately adorned. The result is not to highlight it as of special significance in its own right, as has been the case in the other examples. At another level it acts rather to underline the distinctiveness of the associations of the head above the neck and of the heart beneath.

East African styles of adornment also record in considerable detail and precision the social position and the achievements of the wearer. Different styles of ornament, worn on different parts of the body and in varying quantity, are reserved to people who are in or have passed through particular social conditions. These might include circumcision, initiation, courtship, marriage, the birth of children, bereavement and so forth. The use of jewellery in this way is very general and many instances could be cited. Thus amongst the Naga of north-eastern India male decoration was formerly associated in particular with martial success, especially success in head-hunting. Freshly taken heads of enemies were crucial to a number of rites and essential in ensuring both the well-being of the community and the fertility of the land. And those most adept at providing such heads

12 Turkana woman from northern Kenya, with strings of beads massed round the neck, a beaded skirt (here held up by an ostrich-eggshell belt) and other wood, metal and bead ornaments.

earned the right to ornament themselves in a particular way. For example, among some Naga groups men were able to add a fourth band to their cowrie-shell aprons. The right to this distinctive decorative feature might even be extended to men performing other prodigious feats. Thus it has been suggested that in other contexts it might indicate a man having an intrigue with a woman whilst she still lived with her husband, or with two girls having the same name, with two daughters of the same father, or with a mother and daughter.

In each of these cases we are firmly in the world Professor Diogenes Teufelsdrockh identified. Different social states are systematically declared through ornamentation. What is appropriate adornment for individuals with particular achievements or rank is fixed. For this reason there is no self-consciousness in such adornment and no way, therefore, of gauging the character of the inner person from such externals alone. Most ethnic jewellery probably operates in this way, or at least reports of it are so structured as to imply it does. They suggest that jewellery is not conceived as an act of self-expression in any literal sense.

A major exception to this is offered by the traditions of decoration in Papua New Guinea. Here the most spectacular adornment is associated with events at which many people, elaborately ornamented, appear before large numbers of onlookers. The immediate occasion for such display may be ceremonial exchanges, festive gatherings, or the preparations for conducting a warring expedition; but whatever the overt purpose of such large and colourful gatherings, the display itself, accompanied by singing and dancing, is a major focus of interest. Adornment involves donning such items as the plumes of birds or various shell ornaments, and decorating the body itself by rubbing it with charcoal or oil, or painting it. Each element is important and clearly jewellery as such is only part of the display. The stress is on men rather than women decorating, and they invest considerable time and effort in gathering together the relevant materials and preparing themselves. The events may last over a period of time, so different decorations must be assembled for use on successive days. Finally, it is usual for several clans to perform and parade at major occasions as separate groups. There is thus a highly competitive emphasis in the display.

A number of interpretations have been offered of these impressive events. In each case, however, the point is consistently made that decoration and qualities of character are related. It is not that bejewelling the body is seen perhaps as donning a disguise or as an act of beautification with no deeper purpose beyond the aesthetic. For many in the New Guinea Highlands, in the charged competitive atmosphere of these decorative occasions, adornment is seen as bringing out and revealing true conditions. This is not to say that at other times – during courtship, for instance – decoration does not serve more familiar ends. Yet where, as amongst the Wahgi for example, clansmen would be strongly advised against waging war if their decoration was not up to scratch at precombat displays, something more is clearly implied.

In the case of the Wahgi it has been cogently argued that in an unsettled society such as theirs competitive display is one way of testing the relative state of each clan. But this efficacy in the political domain is itself felt to turn on the inner moral condition of those decorated for display. Their moral state is thought to show itself in the quality of their adornment and display. Groups of poorly adorned warriors are admonished against fighting because they would surely lose. Short of being 'dressed to kill', the imperfect state of their decoration reveals them rather as dressed 'to be killed'. Here, therefore, the assemblage of jewellery and adornment, and how it appears on the cosmetically treated bodies of clansmen, is felt by the thousand or more spectators at larger displays to mirror the moral condition of the clan. Decoration does not impress by virtue of its intrinsic qualities alone but also by virtue of those inhering in the clan itself.

Similar general observations have been made of the peoples living in the Mt Hagen area. For Hageners decoration is at one level disguise, for it is seen as important that in display the first effect is of the decoration. To achieve this the personal identity of individual performers is to an extent effaced and the focus of attention should be the ornamentation, the external objects deployed upon the body rather than the body itself. This seems to be the most extreme use of jewellery and body decoration as described

13 Wahgi men, from Papua New Guinea's Western Highland Province, decorated for their Pig Festival. The visual effects are achieved by a number of means, of which the wearing of jewellery is but one. The character and quality of the decoration is regarded as revealing the dancer's inner moral condition.

above. The adornment dazzles and impresses in the best of displays to the extent that the individual identity of the wearer is successfully suppressed. Yet paradoxically, in a way that had not occurred even to Teufelsdrockh, Hageners regard such successful decoration not as the ultimate in disguise but as the ultimate in revelation. As with the Wahgi, one element in the process of decorative concealment is to lose the individual within the group with whom he performs so that their overall qualities should emerge. Hageners, however, also see the masking of the outer person as a means of bringing forth the inner self. Hidden and basic capacities, desires and intentions are revealed in decoration. Indeed, people who are in an uncertain state, who are ill or have suffered misfortune and bereavement, do not display. To do so, attempting to hide their condition, would be ill-advised, for there is a continuity between inner states and the character of decoration. A good display, one which is admired by the spectators, imparts both prestige and spiritual well-being. Those who seek to cover up their condition, however, inevitably produce a bad display and receive a reputation as 'rubbish men', revealed by the inadequacies of their adornment in their true colours.

In the end this is what many in the self-conscious modern world also seek: a form of decoration through wearing jewellery, as through other cosmetic acts, which is in the most immediate sense an act of *self*-decoration. It is worth recalling that the words 'mask' and 'mascara' are related. Adorning, even in the language used to describe it, is identified as an act of concealment – hiding blemishes, highlighting one area of the body at the expense of another. More importantly, however, some have also begun to identify adornment as a disguise of the true self. The growth of interest in ever more eclectic styles of decoration can be seen as part of the search thereby initiated for more individual, more personal forms of self-expression. To that extent the topic of ethnic jewellery is no longer one of exclusive interest to the anthropologist.

I

Africa

◆

14 Bashima woven grass arm ornaments from northern Nigeria. Much traditional African jewellery was made from perishable organic materials and so did not last long. The natural colours of these armlets show the subtle range of tones available before the introduction of glass beads.

The most obvious and striking feature of African jewellery is its almost universal use. One has only to glance through a collection of photographs of African peoples to see that few, if any, are without a necklace or ear-rings, anklets, armlets or waist beads. Body ornaments and decorations are found in every part of the continent and among all linguistic and social groups. The history of jewellery in Africa reaches far back into the prehistoric past; an oval bone pendant from Redeyef, Tunisia, the earliest firm evidence of self-adornment, is thought to be about 15,000 years old. The use of organic materials – bone, horn, hair, wood, roots, seeds and so on – continues very ancient traditions. Even today some Maasai warriors still wear a form of neckband made from a strip of fresh goat's stomach lining. It is ornamented with fragrant seeds which are pressed onto it while it is still naturally sticky, and is held in place by string; at the centre front is a perforated disc made from the shell of a crocodile's egg.

Organic materials generally perish rapidly, and little remains from an early date, but in a cave on the Njoro River, Kenya, used from about 1000 BC as a cremation cemetery, thousands of tiny beads made from sedge seeds have been found, together with beads made from nuts and naturally hollow bird bones, as well as bone and ivory pendants, and stone beads made from a variety of coloured hardstones. The seed beads far outnumbered the other finds, probably indicating the comparative ease with which they could be made. According to the excavators of Njoro River Cave, identical beads were being produced until recently by the Bagishu of the north-east slopes of Mt Elgon; they estimated that a single bead could be made in five minutes.

Straw is also used elsewhere as the simplest of jewellery. The women of the Middle Niger area of northern Nigeria wear pieces of guinea-corn stalk through holes in their ear-lobes. Among the Bashima of this area grasses, naturally red and dark brown, were woven into patterned ribbons which were then sewn together to form armbands and wristlets. The Kikuyu of Kenya made necklaces and armlets from grasses braided around fibre cores or incorporating hollow cylindrical grass stalks cut to equal lengths and suspended from a length of fibre.

Other organic materials are widely used. In many parts of the continent large flat seeds

15 Maasai neck ornament, Kenya, which includes a complete Conus shell disc, from which hangs a fringe of handmade iron chains. The iron penannular ring is covered with leather, and decorated with imported glass seed beads. Conus shell discs have been high-status ornaments since at least the 5th century AD, and were traded far inland, where their value was much greater than on the coast.

are polished and pierced for use as pendants. In the West African forests young girls will polish the pear-shaped seeds of the oil palm till they are a lustrous black, drill them at the tip and wear them around their necks on lengths of string, sometimes made from the white fibres of the pineapple leaf.

Marine shell, particularly the cowrie and Conus, has long been highly valued for personal adornment in Africa. The cowrie and Conus are species of marine gastropods, originating in the tropical and sub-tropical waters off the East African coast. From an early date they were traded great distances into the interior of the continent and beyond, and have been widely used as currency, as well as for decoration. Cowrie shells could easily be adapted for use in jewellery. The dome of the shell could be ground or chipped away, allowing a string to be passed through the hole thus created and then through the natural opening; in some areas two small holes were drilled through the dome of the shell for threading.

Ornaments made from Conus shell were also believed to act as powerful charms. It is said that the Machinga people, living on the Tanzanian coast near Lindi, revere the Conus shell so highly that they will throw away a whole catch of fish in which one has been found. Only in Angola is the shell said to be worn complete; more usually ornaments of Conus are found in the form of discs, made by cutting off the circular end of the shell. The disc is worked flat and smooth, apart from the natural spiral of the shell, which forms a raised ornament; it is then perforated through the centre.

These ornaments are called *vibangwa*, and for centuries they have been a major element of Central African jewellery, found in Kenya, Tanzania, Zambia and Zaire. They have always been indicators of the high status and wealth of their owners, and were also used as a medium of exchange: in 1854 two *vibangwa* were the price of a slave. *Vibangwa* were often worn on the head, attached to bands of red cloth or leather, or incorporated into necklaces, worn as pendants, or even tied onto the arm or leg. Triangular *vibangwa* could be made by halving or quartering the discs and grinding the piece to the required shape. Genuine Conus shell ornaments are now very rare. Copies have been produced since the 1890s, when the British administration in East Africa flooded the area with Czech-made porcelain imitations, and in the recent past cheap red and blue plastic mass-produced *vibangwa* have become very popular.

Among the earliest known examples of African jewellery are beads made from ostrich-eggshell. They have been made and worn in all parts of Africa where the raw material was available, and are still made today in Sudan and Southern Africa. The San of

16 San ostrich-eggshell bead necklace, Southern Africa. The beads are interspersed with thin discs of leather and threaded on a hide thong. Although the San hunters and gatherers of the Kalahari Desert are among the least encumbered peoples in the world, carrying few possessions as they change camping place frequently, the women make and wear these long sinuous necklaces – this example is 45 inches long.

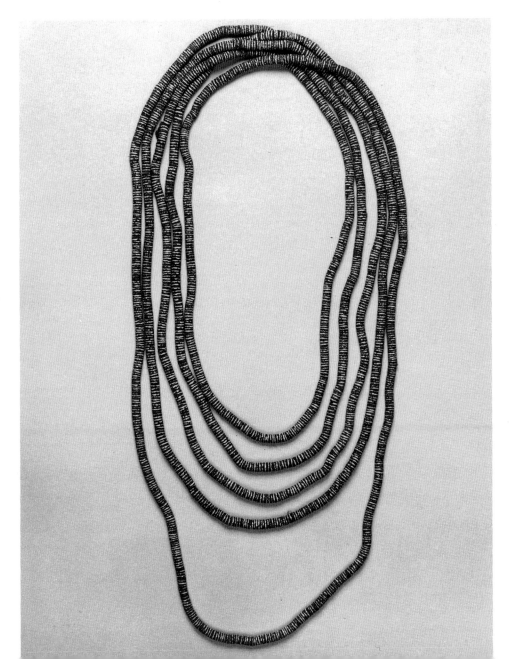

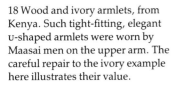

17 Maasai horn snuff-box, from Kenya. Its leather lid is decorated with handmade iron chains and glass seed beads. Snuff containers are worn by Maasai elders on long iron chains around their neck. In this case iron tweezers are provided, attached to the chain.

the Kalahari Desert still value their traditional ostrich-eggshell beads more highly than other ornaments. They are made and worn by the women, who thread them into wide headbands and long necklaces; five or six of these necklaces might be worn, reaching to the navel.

Bone, ivory and wood have, in all probability, been used to make lip- and nose-plugs since the earliest times. In northern Ghana, among the Lobi, old women still wear small wooden or bone discs inserted through a hole in their upper lip. Women among the Makonde of Mozambique formerly had both lips pierced from about the age of five years: at first a small piece of grass was worn through the holes, which were gradually enlarged. By the end of their lives mature women were wearing concave ebony discs 2 inches or more in diameter. The Maasai and other people of East Africa wore large cylindrical wooden or ivory plugs, about 3 inches long, hanging vertically through the vastly stretched lobes of their ears. Some of the wooden ones are decorated with tiny coloured glass beads fixed into the surface.

Over most of Africa the horns of wild antelope were used as containers for mystically powerful materials. Sometimes such horns were incorporated into the necklaces worn by chiefs, priests and hunters, all men whose jewellery had the function of providing magical protection as well as showing their status. Horn and other organic materials could also be made into objects which served both as jewellery and as utilitarian containers. The Zulu and related peoples of Southern Africa carved tiny snuff-boxes out of horn or wood which they wore as adornments pushed through holes in their ear-lobes. These little boxes were often decorated with imported glass beads. Animal teeth, particularly the canines of large carnivores, were worn threaded as ornaments and among the Kikuyu the vertebrae of small mammals and snakes were strung on leather thongs to form sinuous necklaces.

Elephant ivory, too, was often supposed to possess magical qualities. Ornaments of ivory were frequently worn to indicate status. Among the Dinka of southern Sudan, for example, flat armlets or bracelets signified the owner's wealth; delicately carved ivory ornaments were worn by the richer members of the communities in much of Central,

18 Wood and ivory armlets, from Kenya. Such tight-fitting, elegant u-shaped armlets were worn by Maasai men on the upper arm. The careful repair to the ivory example here illustrates their value.

19 *Above* Ivory armlets, Benin, decorated with designs carved in very high relief of kings with coral bead regalia, and elephants. They were probably carved by members of the sculptors' guild for the king himself during the greatest years of the Benin Kingdom, in the 16th century.

20 *Opposite* Amber necklace with a silver pendant, from Somalia. Amber is greatly esteemed in Somalia for its healing properties and large amber necklaces with ornate silver crescent- or bar-shaped pendants are valuable in women's dowries. The silverwork in this example is similar to the work of Yemeni craftsmen.

Southern and Eastern Africa. Ivory was similarly treasured in the kingdoms of tropical Africa, where its association with royalty gave it an added dimension. In Benin, Nigeria, under the patronage of the Oba, or king, the sculptors' guild produced intricately carved ivory ornaments of high quality for the Oba's ceremonial regalia, including belts, masks, plaques and armlets.

Amber and coral were also valued in some parts of the continent for their decorative qualities and for the magical and healing properties they were believed to possess. Coral from the western Mediterranean, presumably acquired from Portuguese traders, was used in the impressive coral-bead regalia of the Obas of Benin. Branch coral found off the coast of Algeria is found in the jewellery of the Berbers of the Maghreb in north-west Africa. It was worn particularly by children for its protective powers.

Amber (fossilised resin) was highly prized in some areas as a symbol of status. Some came from as far afield as the Baltic, the world's major source of amber, and was traded via the Mediterranean, then across the Sahara to the savannah lands of West Africa, or through Egypt and the Red Sea to the Horn of Africa. Copal, a semi-fossilised resin similar to amber was also traded. Copal from Senegal was used by the Berbers, and the Somalis used copal from Zanzibar. The large amber beads worn, for example, by the Dogon and the Fulani of Mali, and by the Somali make a striking and highly conspicuous display of wealth.

The use of hardstones for making beads can be traced back to at least 8000 BC, as finds

21 Fulani woman, Mali, wearing voluminous gold ear-rings. They have been beaten from a solid bar of metal and then bound with red silk or wool thread where they pass through the ear-lobe. Elsewhere in her ear, and sewn into her hair, are small gold rings, and on her fingers she wears cast-silver and polished agate rings.

from Zambia show. In West Africa stone beads and bracelets have been made from at least 3000 BC. Large numbers of these were probably made near outcrops of suitable, attractively coloured hardstone. Among the likely sources of these items are Gao, Niger (pink quartz), Eguei Zouma, Libya (amazonite), Wiawso, Ghana (black and pink hornblende-porphyry), Tilemsi, Mali (cornelian), Arakat, Mali (red flint). Many stone beads still in use today may have originated from these sources hundreds of years ago, having been repeatedly lost, found and re-used.

The trade in hardstones could cover great distances; beads of white agate worn by the Fulani women of northern Nigeria, and triangular pendants of cornelian much valued by the peoples of the savannah, were imported from as far away as India. On a more local scale amazonite and shells from Mauritania, and copal from Senegal, were traded across the Sahara and used by the Berbers of the southern Maghreb (Morocco); these were combined with coral and silver to produce jewellery of a distinctive and flamboyant style. The cost of imported hardstone beads must always have been high; and from the time of the earliest farmers stone beads have been strung together with less costly and less laboriously made seed, shell and clay beads. Coloured glass has long been used as a cheaper alternative for the expensive hardstones, coral and amber.

The development of metalworking techniques added a new dimension to the range of materials either found and worked locally or imported, and greatly enlarged the repertoire of African jewellers. The basic techniques used are hammering into sheet metal, drawing metal into fine wire, and casting. Some of the most impressive sheet-
21 metal jewellery can be found among the Fulani of Mali, where wealth is displayed in the

32

22 Kamba neck-ring, Kenya. The ten concentric rings are made of white metal wire with decorative borders of coloured glass beads.

form of the large amber beads and unwieldy gold ear-rings worn by the women. These ear-rings are made by beating sheet gold into thin blades and twisting them into shape. They may have some incised decoration, but their value lies in the sheer weight of gold: the value of these ear-rings can be considerable.

Nearly all this gold jewellery has disappeared in recent years: the great drought in the Sahel has forced the Fulani to sell it to stay alive. Some women now wear copies of their solid gold ear-rings made of copper covered by a thin wash of gold. Even cheaper copies of traditional forms have been made in new materials: craftsmen make baked clay shapes and wrap them in imported gold-coloured nylon thread. What was once an exclusive source of pride and wealth has been replaced by ornaments costing a few pennies and available to all.

It is probable that this pattern of copying gold and other substances in cheaper materials has a long history. In the Mopti area of Mali ear-rings, pendants and nose-rings made of cut straw stuck over wax forms have been made since at least 1900. Sometimes the straw is dyed yellow with local potassium, while green and red European ink is used to colour areas to look like local embroidered leather. This ink has replaced local dyes. The straw shines through these translucent colourings and the overall effect is of beautiful and delicate gold filigree work.

In East and Southern Africa much of the jewellery is made from iron or copper wire. This method literally stretches the material to its fullest extent and allows a small quantity of metal to be displayed to maximum effect. The traditional techniques of drawing wire have been used for centuries: tools found in tombs dating to the fourteenth century AD at

Ingombe Ilede, Zaire, and Great Zimbabwe, are similar to those in use until recently in parts of Uganda and among the Venda of South Africa.

Wire may be used in a number of ways to make jewellery. Sometimes medium-gauge wire is simply formed into circles and the ends twisted together to form a light bangle; many such bangles may be worn on the arms or legs. Heavier-gauge iron or copper wire may be coiled to form torcs, armlets and bracelets. Fine wire can be wound around a central core of grass, plant fibres or hair; this technique is still practised among the Venda and other groups in South Africa. Sometimes small glass or brass beads are strung onto these light-weight metal-covered bangles and anklets, or small circlets of sheet brass are clenched onto them. A skilled craftsman can make up to a hundred of these bangles during a day's work; each bangle can be completed in three to five minutes. Venda women may wear hundreds of such bangles: about a hundred made from iron wire next to the ankle, two hundred of brass or copper further up the leg, and equally large numbers on the arms.

Among the Celi and Nzikobanyanka peoples of Burundi metal was used to decorate traditional wooden archers' bracelets, cylinders of wood 1½–6 inches thick and up to 8 inches in external diameter. Cone-shaped pieces of metal like nails are hammered into the wood to give the appearance on the surface of little metal discs. Traditionally copper was used, though today aluminium from melted down old saucepans or car parts is more common. Another decorative technique involves inlaying thin strips of metal into narrow grooves carved in the surface of the wooden bracelet. Small rectangular metal plaques, their edges bent at right angles to the decorative face, may also be hammered into the wood like staples. These archers' bracelets are quite expensive items of jewellery; an undecorated bracelet may cost a goat or a sheep, while one with copper ornamentation is valued at five iron hoes.

The massive cast-metal jewellery produced by groups in Central and West Africa (including the Celi and Nzikobanyanka) provides yet another quite different style of ornamentation. Among the Kongo of Zaire the women adorned themselves with the maximum possible number of neck-, arm- and ankle-rings. These might easily weigh 20

23 *Above* Coiled metal armband from Kenya. Maasai women are famous for their brilliantly coloured glass bead jewellery, but on important occasions, particularly weddings, more elaborate metal jewellery is required. The bride's parents provide her with thick white metal wire, which is wound tightly around the arms and legs.

24 *Right* Massive penannular armlet or anklet from the Congo, made in very heavy cast brass.

25 Brass penannular armlet from northern Nigeria, cast by the lost-wax technique, which was well developed in West Africa. The rope-pattern and half-spirals were made from fine threads of wax.

or 30 pounds, giving the wearer a distinguished bearing but making movement difficult and affected. Women who wore these heavy pieces of jewellery were not necessarily exempted from carrying burdens or working in the fields, but were presumably happy to suffer in order to display such conspicuous wealth. The neck-rings worn by the Kongo weigh at least 3 pounds. The older neck-rings were cast in two pieces and had mortice-and-tenon joints, held together by a brass pin. They were abundantly decorated with incised designs. Modern neck-rings are penannular, made from a single piece of brass using a one-piece open mould; technologically and artistically they are of inferior quality to the older type.

Anklets may consist of simple brass rings made of bent and hammered wire, or may be cast penannular rings. The most outstanding anklets are heavy, solid or hollow pieces, weighing more than 6 pounds and some even over 20 pounds. Indeed, before 1930 an old lady from the Tumba region is recorded as wearing an anklet weighing 33 pounds. Like the older type of neck-rings, these heavy ankle ornaments are generally cast in two pieces.

In the West African kingdoms the technique of lost-wax casting was adopted to produce ornaments of great sophistication and intricacy. Benin became a centre of brass-casting, and the regalia of the Oba and his courtiers included many fine cast-brass ornaments. But from Ghana comes perhaps the most spectacular metal jewellery made in

26 *Right* Two royal gold finger- or toe-rings from Asante, Ghana (19th century), cast by the lost-wax technique.

27 *Opposite* Coral and glass bead necklace, with silver chains, coins, an engraved central disc-shaped pendant, a filigree spherical bead, and enamelled plaques. The two square plaques with blue, green and red cloisonné enamel are characteristic of the work of the Kabyle smiths of northern Algeria.

26 all of Black Africa, produced for the kings and chiefs of the kingdom of Asante. The magnificence of the Asante kings and their court almost overwhelmed many white visitors who recorded breathless descriptions of what they encountered at the capital at Kumase. Much of the impact of this deliberately impressive display resulted from the vast amounts of gold with which the Asantehene (overall king) and his officials adorned themselves. In public appearances the weight of gold that the king wore on his arms, wrists and fingers was so great that he was obliged to rest his hands on the heads of small boys who stood before him.

The gold was panned and mined locally, and its use was closely controlled by the court. Specialist craftsmen developed great skill in lost-wax casting, creating pieces of 156 enormous delicacy and fineness. Many of the castings they made served a dual function: their subject matter called to mind proverbs or sayings which represented traditional wisdom while, at the same time, they impressed the ordinary people and visitors by their sheer richness and profusion. The kings were careful to control the use of gold by those beneath them and to restrict the way it could be worn. Slaves, at the bottom end of society, were forbidden to possess gold jewellery of any sort, while the amount, size and form of gold ornaments used by office-holders at each level of the hierarchy was strictly determined.

In areas where the influence of Islam has been strong silver has traditionally been preferred to gold. Silver is thought by Muslims to be pure and propitious. The Berbers believed that combined with certain stones silver could be particularly beneficial: for example, topaz (against jaundice), emerald (against snake bites) and rubies (good for the heart). Berber silversmiths mastered the techniques of filigree, enamelling and cloisonné work, which are thought to have been brought from Spain by immigrant Jewish silversmiths. Among the Kabyle of northern Algeria, Jewish silversmiths have special-165 ised in cloisonné enamelling, traditionally preferring the colours green, yellow and blue.

The common forms of jewellery worn include diadems and head-dresses, anklets, necklaces and fibulae.

Silver coins are also much used in jewellery in these areas. In the savannah lands old French and Austrian coins, originally imported into Africa as currency, have been used by women as hair ornaments. The silver from melted down coins has also been reused in ornaments for the hair. Among the poorer people the silver coins are exchanged for less valuable coins, or even glass beads and buttons.

In Morocco coins are joined together by links and chains to form elaborate breast

28 Silver head ornament, Talsint, Morocco: engraved plaques with niello decoration linked by chains and rings.

ornaments and head-dresses. In southern Morocco the profusion of valuable jewellery collected eagerly by women of the Tissint people makes a colourful and flamboyant display, combining coral, amber and amazonite with silver beads decorated with granulation and filigree and large quantities of silver coins.

Among many peoples of Eastern and Southern Africa, notably the Maasai, Samburu and Kikuyu, the Zulu and the Swazi, a completely different and extremely complex style of personal adornment has been developed, based on one of the simplest components of jewellery, the monochrome bead, used in overwhelming profusion. Tens of thousands of tiny glass seed beads may be strung or sewn to make elaborately structured and multi-coloured ornaments. The development of these distinctive forms of personal ornament rests on the use of imported materials: the explosion in multi-coloured beadwork came in the early nineteenth century, when coloured beads from Europe became widely available for the first time.

The jewellery itself, the way it is worn, the choice and combination of colours all convey social messages. The beadwork of the Zulu, in particular, is so elaborate and yet so precisely codified that it has often been called a 'language'. The Zulu and Swazi mark important stages in their physical and social development from infancy onwards by

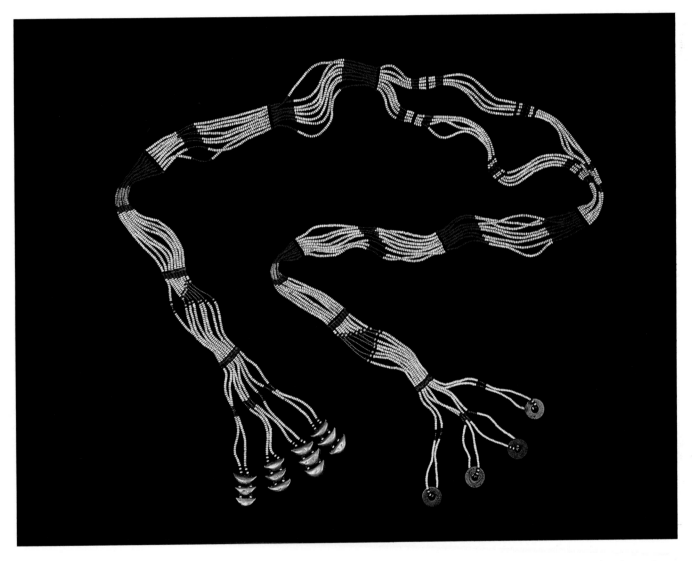

29 Kamba bead ornament from Kenya. The multi-coloured strands of glass seed beads have pendant terminals of crescent-shaped aluminium beads – made from melted down saucepans – and bronze coins.

wearing beads of different colours. For example, when a girl first falls in love, she makes a necklace, a single string of beads of one colour, which she gives to her lover, and makes for herself a matching set of wrist, ankle and waist beads. The wearing of these ornaments by both partners publishes the news of their liaison. Meeting a group of Zulu girls one could, therefore, tell who was in love, who was too young for affairs and who had progressed beyond her first lover, the last stage signalled by the fact that the girl may wear any type or colour of bead and make them into sewn or threaded patterned bead ornaments.

Zulu and Swazi girls spend some of their leisure sitting in groups sewing rectangular

30 South African beadwork. The patterned beadwork of such peoples as the Zulu and Xhosa conveys specific messages, often transmitted by the colours used, by their juxtaposition, motifs and overall design. Small rectangular panels, or 'love letters' (*top row, centre*) are made by teenage girls for the young men of their fancy; different colours are peculiar to each locality. Beads may decorate many objects too – aprons (*lower row*), bottles and armlets (*top row*).

pieces of patterned beadwork which they give to their lovers. These ornaments convey specific messages to the young men, since the colours of the beads used, their juxtaposition, the motifs depicted and the overall design all have definite significance, though their meanings vary from region to region. The principal design motifs are squares, diamonds, straight lines, zig-zags and lozenges, arranged in symmetrical, geometric patterns. Messages as complicated as 'I say this with an open white heart. I say, ''Oh for the dove that picks food in the yard at your kraal.'' I envy also the one who enjoys your fireplace', can be conveyed by beads. This message could be 'written' by stringing beads as follows: five white, three blue, five white, three red, five white, three pink, repeated twice. It is hardly surprising that the recipients of these 'love letters' often have to consult their sisters for interpretations of the encoded messages. Because the girls sit in groups while making the beadwork patterns, and consult one another about the messages they are sewing, they find decipherment easy.

Married women usually wear several hoop-like circular-sectioned necklaces made by wrapping strings of beads tightly around thick fibre cords; they also adopt a distinctive head-dress consisting of a flared, red ochre-covered or red beaded crown with a

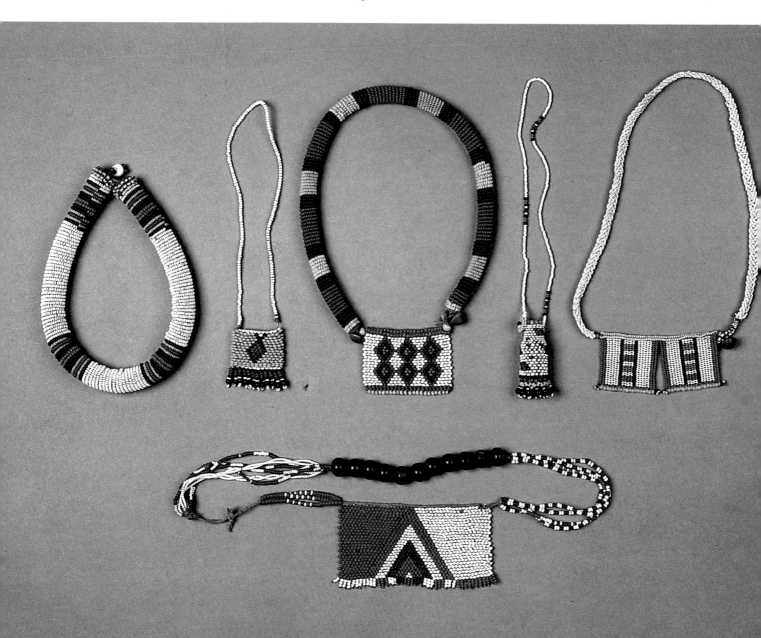

31 Samburu girl with her bead jewellery. Beadwork is the primary decorative art among many Eastern and Southern African peoples. Extremely elaborate forms of adornment have developed since the early 19th century. A young woman of the Samburu is considered naked and ugly if she is seen without at least four or five pounds of beads.

bead-covered band around its base. When a woman is widowed she changes the colour scheme of her jewellery, making black the predominant colour in the design.

Other peoples who make great use and display of beadwork have not developed such a precise 'language', but beads can still represent a method of communication in these societies. Among the Samburu of Kenya it is immediately possible to deduce a person's status from the beadwork he or she is wearing: whether he is an uncircumcised youth, a warrior, an elder or a priest; or whether she is a virgin, a marriageable girl, a married woman, a mother, the mother of a warrior, or a woman past childbearing age. Beads do not just constitute decoration for the Samburu, they display a person's humanity, their social state, for to be without several pounds of beads is tantamount to being naked. Samburu women wear massive ensembles of beads around their shoulders and necks, usually made from thousands of small, single-coloured glass seed beads. The great collars of beads make the head look as if it is lifted high, and frame the face, concentrating attention upon it. The Samburu ideal of feminine beauty, though, emphasises the ornaments, not the person wearing them. When asked what makes a beautiful woman the reply would probably be: 'She will have beads right up to her chin. This is what makes her beautiful'. In fact, a pretty girl will be given many gifts of jewellery by her suitors, and so her ornaments reinforce her attractiveness. The male concept of beauty and personal adornment is different. Narrow bands or beads worn as circlets and bandoliers around the head, neck, chest, waist, arms and legs enhance the natural elegance of the men's shiny, well-built, slim bodies, while the women's jewellery alters the body shape and makes great use of large masses of beads and colour contrasts within the collars and ear-rings.

The Maasai of Kenya and Tanzania, who are related culturally and linguistically to the Samburu, have similar ideals of masculine and feminine beauty, and are equally lavish in their use of beadwork. Maasai women wear distinctive ear-pendants from perforations in their ear-lobes; these long, tongue-shaped ornaments are made from leather decorated with sewn polychrome beadwork designs. Both boys and girls have their ears pierced before circumcision; the perforation is gradually stretched by inserting increasingly large ear-plugs, leaving a distended loop of flesh which incorporates the beaded ear ornament. For boys the resulting loop is usually smaller; men tend to wear penannular metal ear-rings with trumpet-shaped terminals or coil a string of small glass beads around the core of skin. Both sexes often have other perforations in the ear-lobe, sometimes halfway up the ear but more commonly near the top. From these are suspended lighter, more delicate beaded ear ornaments.

Another characteristic item of jewellery is the stiff, flat, beaded collar worn by Maasai women of marriageable age. These collars are made of glass beads threaded onto wire, the individual strands joined to build up a light, flexible framework. Red, white and blue beads predominate, although yellow, orange, green and black beads are often used in smaller quantities. The head-dresses worn by the Maasai women consist of three or more strings of beads encircling the head, which is shaved; these may be joined at the front by a band of beadwork, often decorated with mother-of-pearl buttons. Sometimes loops of silver or gilt chain hang from the head-dress across the cheeks. A beadwork aigrette may be worn rising from the front of the head-dress and sloping backwards over the skull. Strings of beads are wound around the wrists to make tight-fitting armlets.

Maasai men also wear jewellery, though not in such great profusion. *Moran*, or warriors, wear colourful bandolier-like bead ornaments across the chest and snugly fitting bands of striped beadwork encircle the neck like chokers. Of the many types of beaded jewellery made by the Maasai (there are at least forty words in the Maasai language for distinct types of beaded decorations), the *moran* treasure the arm and leg

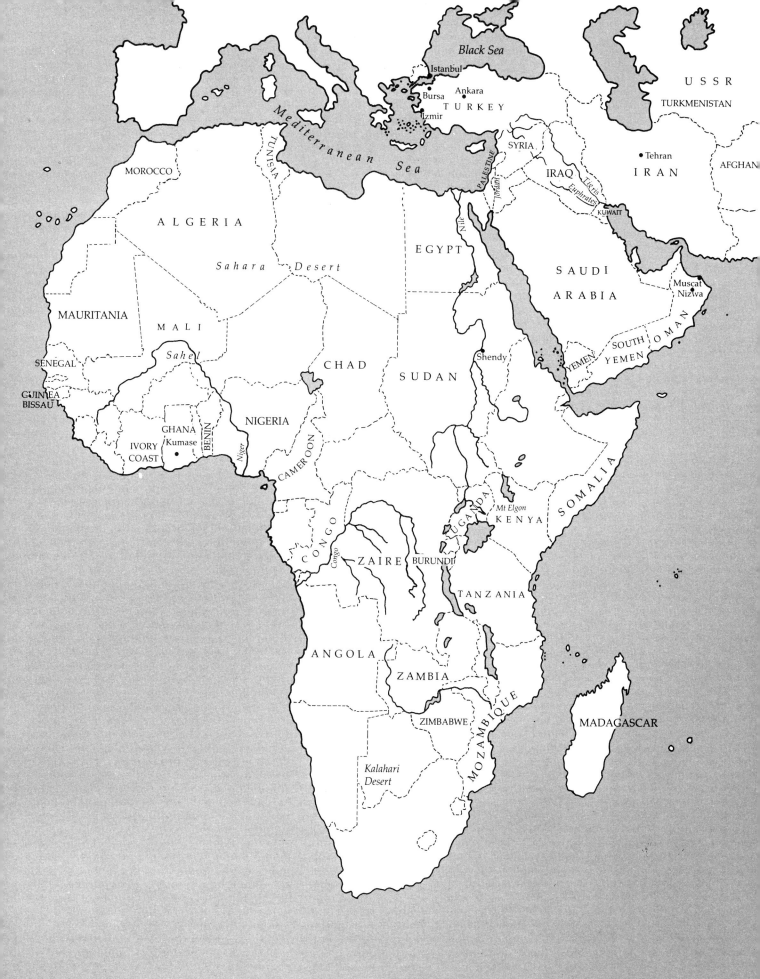

Black Sea

Istanbul
Bursa • Ankara
Izmir • T U R K E Y

SYRIA
PALESTINE
Jordan
IRAQ
Tigris
Euphrates
KUWAIT

USSR
TURKMENISTAN

• Tehran
I R A N
AFGHAN

Mediterranean Sea

MOROCCO

TUNISIA

A L G E R I A

Sahara   Desert

EGYPT

Nile

SAUDI
ARABIA

Muscat •
Nizwa

MAURITANIA

M A L I

Sahel

CHAD

SUDAN

Shendy •

YEMEN

SOUTH
YEMEN

O M A N

SENEGAL

NIGERIA

GUINEA
BISSAU

GHANA
Kumase •

IVORY
COAST

BENIN

Niger

CAMEROON

CONGO

Congo

ZAIRE

BURUNDI

UGANDA

Mt Elgon

K E N Y A

S O M A L I A

T A N Z A N I A

A N G O L A

ZAMBIA

ZIMBABWE

MOZAMBIQUE

MADAGASCAR

*Kalahari
Desert*

Map 1 *Left* Africa and the Middle East, showing the principal place-names mentioned in the text.

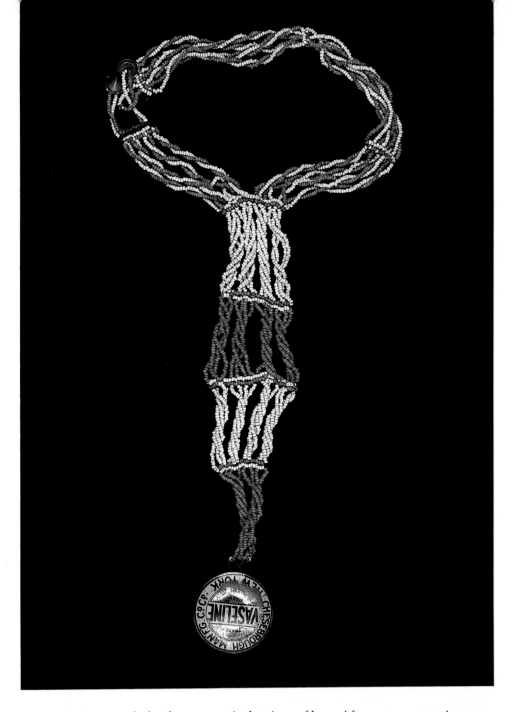

32 Many European objects, often discarded by their original owners, have been incorporated as exotic items into African jewellery. Here a Vaseline tin has been turned into a pendant for a glass bead necklace, from the Tolso region of South Africa.

bands which are made for them as particular signs of love. After years as warriors men become junior elders and are allowed to marry. They shed their long plaited tresses and much of the alluring jewellery which they have worn to attract the girls. Elders soon develop a dignified bearing suitable to their status, and wear less flamboyant jewellery. One of the signs of an elder is the beaded snuff container which he wears around his neck, always given to him by his eldest daughter.

Africans have always been receptive to new materials for use in making their jewellery. In the last century there has been a vast flood of these into the continent, outweighing anything known from the past. While glass beads were traded across the Sahara from Roman times, and then by sea following the earliest European contact, literally tons of these, mostly made in Austria, the Low Countries and Czechoslovakia, were shipped to Africa in the colonial period. The colours of these beads were far brighter than anything seen previously. In some regions of Southern and Eastern Africa they led to an outburst of creativity, in which many items of dress and adornment were decorated all over in elaborate ways. But other imported materials also found a use. Aluminium from

33 *Opposite* Traditional African jewellery is sometimes adapted to suit European taste and fashions. Here typical Asante gold discs and beads have been strung on a chain to produce a symmetrical, European-style necklace.

containers and old car fittings was melted down and cast into rings, beads and pendants. Copper and brass wire were twisted together to make bi-coloured bracelets. European brass buttons have been sewn onto cloth or strung with beads to provide adornment in most parts of the continent. Imported bottles were crushed and the glass remelted to make beads. The basic requirement in most of these cases was that the material should be colourful and shiny. Among the Balanta of Guinea Bissau it has become a fashion for pubescent boys to wear head fillets made of carefully drilled scraps of ceramic bathroom tile strung on lengths of rubber cut from old inner tubes. Among the Xhosa a woman was observed wearing a bead necklace incorporating mother-of-pearl buttons and a silver salt spoon, possibly for use as a snuff spoon. Also from Southern Africa are examples of small circular tins being strung on bead necklaces. One originally contained Vaseline and one a medicinal balm. Early in the century some Maasai were wearing ear-plugs made from rolled-up newspaper. The recent spread of plastics has also deeply affected African creativity. Many pieces of coloured plastic are now recyled into pendants, shaped into finger-rings or made into hair adornments.

While Europe has been providing material for use as jewellery, it has also been stripping Africa of most of its traditional forms of personal ornamentation. Beads of all descriptions, some of which may be hundreds of years old, have been bought up by tourists and collectors, as well as by jewellery designers, and removed for ever from the continent. Many of the cast-metal neck-rings and anklets are no longer made, and ones dating from two or three generations ago are eagerly sought by Western collectors, not for wear, but for display as objects of aesthetic merit. A similar fate has befallen ivory armlets, ear-plugs and many other treasured objects. Africans, of course, have been willing to help meet the growing demands of tourists for what they see as authentic African jewellery. In recent years they have taken to mounting one or two old beads onto strips of leather or discs of wood assuring their gullible buyers that this is a traditional form. Where genuine beads are no longer available newly made imports are used, then given a fake appearance of age by being covered in dirt. Turned ivory beads and roughly polished beads in a wide variety of stones are now imported from India for sale in this way.

Nevertheless, traditional jewellery is still produced in Africa today in a time-honoured manner. The use of natural and locally available materials which can be worked with basic techniques and using simple tools can be traced back millennia. The making of jewellery from metal relies on traditions many hundreds of years old which have produced a rich variety of styles and forms, ranging from simple, fine-wire jewellery to the intricate gold lost-wax castings of West Africa.

The colours of traditional African jewellery can be subdued and subtle: creamy-white shell beads, grey-brown agates, russet cornelians, brown and black seed beads and highly polished ivory which may have been coloured with red palm oil or camwood powder to produce a honey-coloured or reddish-brown patination. Combined with these natural materials, metal jewellery, whether brightly polished with sand to shine and catch the light, or allowed to remain dull yet achieving an attractive patination, echoes the natural, non-synthetic colours of the other ornaments. But the love of vivid colour is also an important part of the story: the profusion of elaborate gold jewellery set against brilliantly coloured textiles worn at the Asante court dazzled the early European visitors; and the jewellery and costume of some of the peoples of Southern and Eastern Africa is impossible to imagine without the masses of brightly coloured tiny beads used to such stunning effect. The inventive and ingenious use of many modern imported materials has increased the range of colour and texture in African jewellery, and testifies to the continuing vitality of an ancient and distinctive tradition.

2

The Middle East

♦

34 Yemeni woman with her bridal jewellery, photographed c. 1980. Here the art of the Yemeni silversmith is displayed to full effect, notably in the elaborate wedding necklace, where the techniques of granulation and applied filigree wire are used to decorate the plaques and amulet containers.

The term 'Middle East' is at most a conveniently flexible label for an area whose historical and cultural traditions are so rich and complex that they elude precise definition. Such qualities are strikingly illustrated in the profusion of styles and techniques found in jewellery. The Middle East encompasses the regions framing the eastern and southern Mediterranean – Turkey, Syria-Palestine, Egypt, North Africa, and their hinterlands of Iraq, Iran and the Arabian peninsula. Through historical circumstance the Middle East extends culturally into the south-east European territories of the former Ottoman Turkish Empire, the Caucasus, Afghanistan, Central Asia and India. Naturally, such a vast area presents a great variation of geography, race and language, unified only to a certain extent by common factors of history and religion.

The Middle East is heir to the highly civilised pre-Islamic kingdoms of Pharaonic Egypt, Assyria-Babylon, Byzantium, Achaemenid and Sassanid Iran. Through diplomacy, trade and, at times, warfare these kingdoms exerted mutually stimulating economic, social and cultural influences on each other, but from the seventh century AD onwards the rapid expansion of Islam into these lands exercised a powerful unifying effect, certainly in terms of spiritual and ethical values. Some regions of the Middle East such as Turkey, the Levant and Egypt have long been accessible to Europe through political and military intervention and commerce. Recently the rapid development of tourism has opened Turkey, Egypt and North Africa to a wide public, while the interior and coastal territories of Arabia have become familiar to a significant European expatriate community recruited for its technical skills. Both tourist and professional public have encouraged a market for the portable products of indigenous tradition, such as jewellery.

Jewellery has always been valued in the Middle East as an attractive personal possession, a status symbol and as a means of financial investment. The materials and techniques employed reflect the economic and social divisions of society. The precious metals of gold and silver have normally been restricted to court and wealthy merchant circles, though people of restricted means did and still do save to invest in family jewellery. Among other metals the use of bronze was widespread. The most sophisticated decorative techniques concentrate on gold and silver: engraving, repoussé work,

47

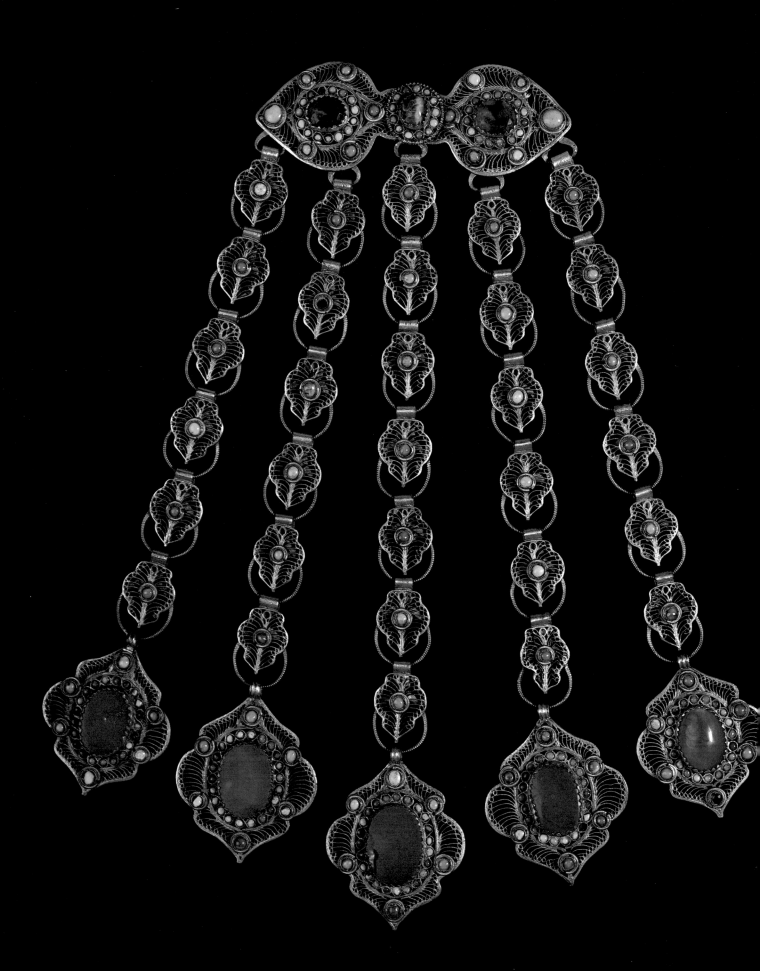

36 *Above* Woman's ear-rings from Kokand, Uzbekistan (USSR) and an amulet-case from Central Asia (late 19th century). Here white metal is gilded, moulded and stamped into chains and pendants which are then decorated with turquoise-blue and orange beads.

35 *Left* Woman's belt buckle, from Russian Turkestan (Kazak, late 19th century). It is made of gold metal with chains of turquoise-studded filigree plaques ending in bold agate-inlaid pendants.

granulation and filigree; decoration of bronze, brass and other base metals is usually confined to motifs worked into the original mould. Other techniques for embellishing jewellery include the application or inlaying of other metals to the base, the use of coloured enamels, either as mosaics or as finely painted designs, and the setting of precious and semi-precious stones into metal mounts, notably diamonds, rubies, emeralds, pearls, turquoises and cornelians.

Jewellery has survived in considerable quantities from the medieval Islamic period of the ninth to eleventh centuries up to modern times, enabling a progression of styles and techniques to be traced. As early as the ninth century gold- and silversmiths were skilled in fashioning light, graceful forms adorned with filigree and set with gemstones. Finds also demonstrate the long survival across a wide geographical span of certain types of personal ornament. Hoards of the eleventh century from as far apart as Tarabia in Tunisia and Chimkent in Central Asia include forms which may still be seen in village jewellery today, such as sheet-gold pendants, decorated with filigree, and massive silver bracelets, pendants and amulets.

Pictorial and written sources yield much valuable information about jewellery and how it was worn. Turkish and Persian paintings show the jewellery in its proper context, and

37 Detail of an ivory belt from the tomb of Selim II at Ayasofya, Turkey (late 16th century). Plaques and finely articulated links of ivory are embellished with spiralling foliage of gold inlay and studded with small rubies and turquoises.

European paintings, engravings and later photographs all provide evidence of jewellery 'in action'. Literary sources bear witness to the value and importance of jewellery in Middle Eastern society. The conventions of Arabic, Persian and Turkish poetry employ lavish descriptions of precious gems as a device of metaphor. Prose accounts of jewellery, such as those left by European travellers to the Middle East, are especially valuable where the original examples have not survived.

All sources agree that the jewellery served a wide range of functions. The most obvious and conspicuous use was as personal adornment, worn by both men and women. All areas of the body could be adorned: the head with ear- and nose-rings; the neck with all manner of necklaces, chokers, pendants; arms, hands, ankles and feet with bracelets, anklets and rings. Closely associated is the use of jewellery as a dress accessory – head-dresses such as crowns, hats, diadems, ornaments intertwined in the hair, plume-holders (aigrettes) placed in turbans, brooches, button fastenings, and gem-encrusted armbands, cuffs, collars and belts. Even weapons may have been regarded as dress accessories, as can be seen by the gilded and jewelled daggers worn with Ottoman Turkish court dress. Jewellery also has symbolic uses in both orthodox and popular Islam; gem-studded cases at the Ottoman court, for example, were to contain relics of the Prophet Muhammad, while at more modest levels are amulets, charms and talismans.

The jewellery of Turkey consistently illustrates a balance of two main traditions, one dominated by the requirements of the Ottoman court culture for luxurious and technically versatile pieces, the other responding to the needs of a more widespread clientele for ornaments of personal and talismanic value. While it is the latter tradition which continues to flourish today, it is the sophisticated jewellery of the Ottoman period which established standards of craftsmanship and design.

The principal source of Ottoman Turkish jewellery is the collection of some six hundred pieces housed today in the Treasury of the Topkapi Palace Museum in Istanbul. The Treasury was formally established by Sultan Mehmet II after his conquest of Constantinople in 1453; its basis was the jewellery of the defeated Byzantine court and of the various Muslim rulers of Anatolia whom the Ottoman Turks had gradually eliminated as they consolidated their power. Control of the gold and silver mines of the Balkan provinces and of the copper reserves of Anatolia ensured a constant supply of raw materials. The Treasury was always regarded as the personal property of the Sultans, who successively enriched it, notably in the sixteenth and seventeenth centuries, by purchase and commission, and by additions through gift and campaign booty. Together the collection represents an incomparable reference source of materials, techniques and forms, which were constantly enriched by the material and human resources of an empire spanning Europe and Asia. Through commissions for the Treasury a nucleus of court workshops was established that recruited craftsmen from all provinces of the empire, which in turn contributed to a blending of jewellery-making traditions. Skilled gold- and silversmiths embellished their products with a variety of techniques: chasing, engraving, repoussé work, as well as intricate filigree and inlays of different metals at various levels of relief. One of the main identifying features of Turkish jewellery was a taste for brilliant colour schemes. These were achieved through the art of the gem-cutter, who fashioned plaques of jade and mother-of-pearl, and inserted diamonds, emeralds, rubies and turquoises, either in their natural state or cabochon-cut, into plain metal settings. Since a pleasing colour effect was all important, diamonds were often set over pieces of red and green metal foil.

The wearing of jewellery by both sexes was restrained and may properly be classified as costume accessory. In the sixteenth and seventeenth centuries it was mainly confined to head-dress ornament, garment fastenings and belts. Indeed, the bold, large-scale patterns of the heavy silk brocades used for costume were sufficiently decorative. The turbans worn by both men and women were embellished with gold ornaments consisting of pointed sockets to hold feathers and plumes, stuck into the turbans and fastened by chains. The belts worn over robes were elegant slender bands or articulated buckles and plaques made of gold, silver, ivory and mother-of-pearl, offering scope for the most refined jeweller's art. Graceful designs of spiralling foliage interlaced with floral motifs were inlaid in gold or rubies and turquoises.

From the eighteenth century onwards more pieces of Ottoman jewellery have survived from a wider range of geographical and social environment. As dress fashions evolved jewellery became lighter and more intricate in design. In women's costume, for example, head-dresses were adorned with jewelled pins and chains, while belts were fastened with large gem-studded clasps. Examples of gold and silver ear-rings of late nineteenth-century date show techniques and forms comparable with those of medieval jewellery. From hoops of drawn metal wire hang graceful crescent-shaped pendants ornamented with filigree coils and drops. Variants of these later jewellery fashions have survived from both Anatolia and the Balkan provinces, showing a blending of urban and local traditions: elaborate circular gold and silver ornaments for pillbox caps, often with fringes of coins, and large belt buckles were distinctive costume accessories.

Modern Turkish jewellery, despite the many social and cultural changes which followed the establishment of the Turkish Republic in 1925, still shows the influence of Ottoman traditions in standards of craftsmanship and design. A steady demand continues among the Turks themselves for valuable jewellery both as gift and as a means of

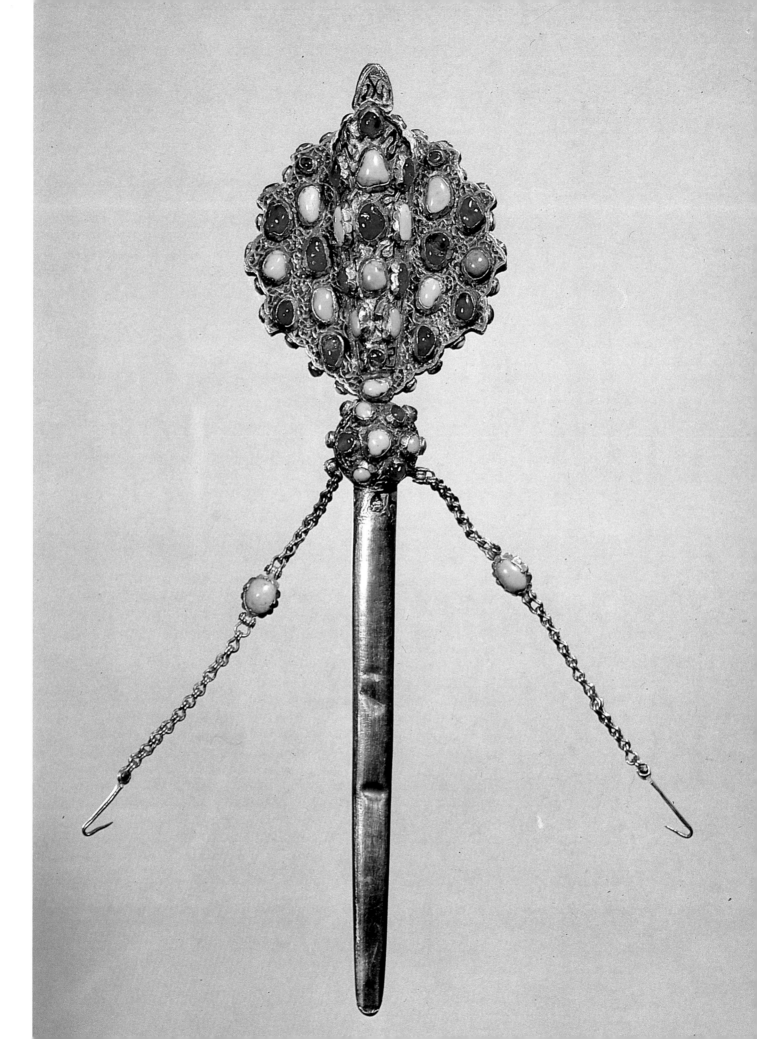

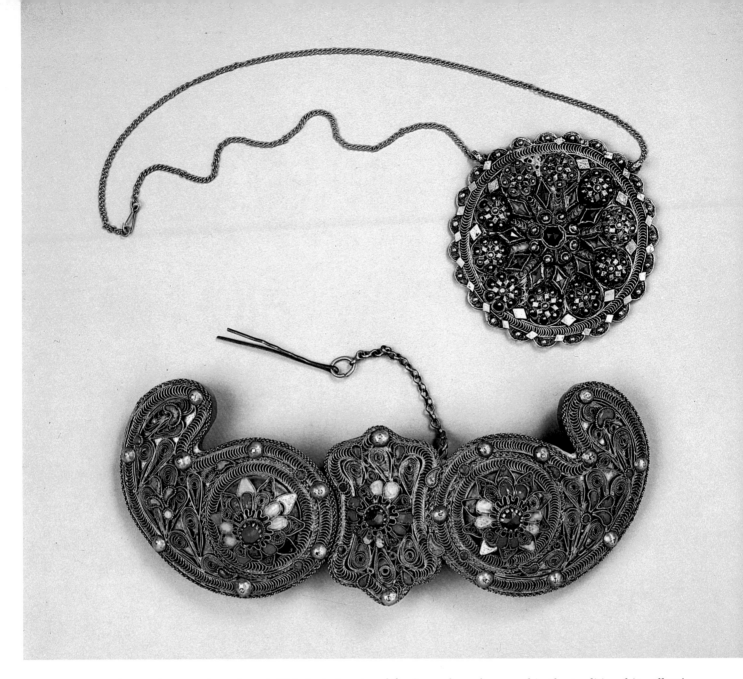

39 *Above* Woman's silver pendant and belt buckle from Bosnia, Yugoslavia (late 19th century). These pieces with their elaborate designs of beaded wire, cloisonné enamel and coloured glass inlay show the influence of Ottoman Turkish taste.

38 *Left* Ottoman Turkish turban ornament (mid-16th century). Gold decorated with niello and encrusted with cabochon-cut turquoises and rubies.

investment. This taste is catered for in modern shops and in the traditional jewellers' quarters of the bazaars. Gold and, to a lesser extent, silver continue to be the preferred metals. In the boutiques of the main cities of Istanbul, Ankara, Izmir and Bursa gold necklaces, bracelets, rings, brooches and ear-rings are fashioned and ornamented with granulation and filigree work. Designs are adapted to the form of European types of jewellery, such as lapel brooches, stud ear-rings and wrist-watches. Especially interesting are modern Turkish designs in which gold and silver are combined with black coral – a striking addition to the traditional repertoire of ruby, emerald and turquoise. The repertoire of gold jewellery has also been extended through archaeological discovery, as many technically brilliant copies are made of Bronze Age finds from Troy, as well as Hellenistic, Roman, Byzantine, Seljuk and Ottoman originals. One type of gold pendant, a popular religious talisman during the eighteenth and nineteenth centuries, illustrates the adaptation of a traditional Ottoman form. Made of sheet gold in teardrop or oval shape with looped filigree borders, these pendants bore Arabic inscriptions from the Qur'ān. They are now made in circular, oval or rectangular shape, and their Qur'ānic inscriptions have been replaced by versions of the *tughra* – a calligraphic device representing the stylised signature of an Ottoman Sultan; threaded onto thin gold chains to

40 Woman's chain necklace from Turkey (mid-20th century): the sheet-gold pendant has a cut and engraved openwork foliate border framing an applied *tughra* motif.

⁴⁰ make handsome necklaces, their function today is purely decorative. Such pendants are sold as frequently in the jewellers' quarter of a traditional bazaar as in a fashionable boutique.

Turkey's rapidly increasing tourist industry has provided new outlets for the jeweller, attracting customers from East and West. The popularity, for example, of Istanbul's Bosphorus suburbs with holiday visitors from Saudi Arabia and the Arab Gulf has resulted in increased custom for the goldsmiths, who also fashion items specifically to suit this Arab taste. The windows of the jewellers' shops of Istanbul's Grand Bazaar are now crowded with ornate gold necklaces whose pendants cover the wearer from neck to waist, and hand jewellery consisting of a ring for each finger and thumb linked by chains to a bracelet. Such jewellery is worn by a bride and her female relatives and guests at traditional weddings. An influx of Western tourists in coastal resorts such as Kusadasi and Bodrum has led to a rapid growth in shopping facilities. Among the leather clothing, ceramics, antiquities and modern jewellery are the familiar gold necklaces with *tughra* pendants, bracelets and rings, as well as attractively designed silver pieces inspired by traditional Turkish village jewellery. These include necklaces and bracelets of chains threaded with turquoise and coral beads, necklets with large alternating beads of silver and amber, and spirally twisted bracelets with snake's head finials.

41 Popular talismans from Turkey (mid-20th century). The glass pendants and glazed pottery tortoise are embellished with 'evil eye' motifs, for protection, and the tortoise also has a pomegranate bead, a symbol of fertility. The glass beadwork pendant with two birds has the inscription *masallah*, 'Praise be to God'.

At certain levels souvenirs made for the tourist market and talismans which reflect the continuity of popular religious belief overlap in an interesting way. One of the most remarkable examples is seen in the flourishing production of blue glass talismans worn as a protection against the evil eye. Traditionally they were pendants of circular or oval shape and made of thick bright-blue glass with a fierce black dotted white pupil applied in relief. This form continues, and may be seen still pinned to the sleeves of babies and young children, but the eye talisman can now be bought in many forms from gift shops and bazaar stalls, and its original protective function has given way to that of a decorative trinket. Another popular talisman made in beadwork, aimed more at a Turkish market though available in tourist shops, is the pendant in the form of a bird. This is made of small coloured beads knotted onto white cotton thread in a fabric which is stretched over a body shape. These birds, either singly or in pairs, are mounted into a beaded frame often inscribed with *masallah*, 'Praise be to God'. They are favourite talismans with long-distance bus- and truck-drivers and may be seen gaily suspended around a vehicle's window and dashboard together with glass eye-beads, festoons of braid and artificial flowers.

A survey of the jewellery traditions of Turkey's large eastern neighbour, Iran, affords opportunities for comparison and contrast. They shared common techniques: Iranian

42 Portrait in oils of Fath Ali Shah (1797–1834) in court costume, by Mihr Ali, 1813, Iran. Pearls, rubies and diamonds are set into gold to create his hat, collar, armbands, cuffs, belt and scabbard.

craftsmen migrated to the Ottoman Court and were also among the prisoners taken by Sultan Selim I after his capture of Tabriz in 1514. Iranian jewellery may broadly be divided between the luxurious products ordered for a court and urban society and the ornaments worn by the complex mixture of rural and nomadic groups; the latter are readily identifiable through their distinctive combinations of metals and gems.

Surviving examples of medieval jewellery from Iran demonstrate a range of forms and a high level of skill in the use of such techniques as filigree work and granulation, and in the cutting and setting of semi-precious stones. Some of this jewellery has parallels in the comparatively modern jewellery of the Türkmen tribes of north-east Iran. From the sixteenth century onwards, after Iran had been brought under the comparatively secure rule of the Safavid Shahs (1501–1732), an increasingly detailed picture of jewellery emerges. Miniature paintings of the sixteenth and seventeenth centuries indicate a lavish use of jewellery in court circles, in contrast to Ottoman Turkish practice. In addition to gem-studded aigrettes, turbans were often decorated with many gold plaques set with rubies and emeralds linked by strings of pearls. Men also wore gold hoop ear-rings and elaborate belts made up of linked gold plaques. A correspondingly abundant quantity of jewellery was worn by women, including diadems of faceted gold pieces and necklaces which ranged from strings of pearls to heavy collars hung with pendants which again have parallels in Türkmen ornament.

The most comprehensive and spectacular source of late historical Iranian jewellery is the collection of the Crown Jewels. The collection was formed in the seventeenth century from inherited gems, purchases, gifts and spoils of war – much as the Ottoman Treasure had been amassed. The turbulence of Iran's history during the eighteenth century meant that they were dispersed, but Nadir Shah (1739–47) brought the collection together again and it was finally inherited by the Qajar Shahs of the nineteenth and early twentieth centuries, who in turn increased its holdings. The Crown Jewels were regarded both as the personal resources of the ruler and as a means of embellishing his person to create an impressive public image.

The materials and techniques employed, while sharing certain features with the jewellery of the Ottoman Turks, reveal fundamental differences in taste which are reinforced by the function of the finished products. Gold was the most favoured metal, but worked in sheet form without any effort at the richness of inlay and filigree techniques found in Ottoman jewellery; it was primarily treated as a base for lavish settings of gemstones or coloured enamels. The gems themselves were cabochon-, rose-, mogul- and brilliant-cut, set in plain mounts and relying for their impact on size and quality. As in Ottoman practice, slips of coloured metal foil were placed behind diamonds to enhance their effect. Iran's access to local and foreign sources of gemstones is reflected in the types represented: diamonds mainly from the Golconda mines of India and, after the 1880s, from South Africa; emeralds from South America; rubies from Burma and Thailand; spinels from Badakhshan; and a plentiful supply of turquoises from the Iranian mines of Meshed and Nishapur. Apart from a greater concentration of gems and the more abundant use of pearls (fished from the waters of the Gulf and off Ceylon), the resulting colour scheme is comparable to that of Ottoman jewellery. A brilliant use of coloured enamels to create subtly painted designs on jewellery and ornaments may perhaps be regarded as the Iranian craftsman's equivalent of the intricate inlay and filigree work of the Ottoman goldsmith.

The dazzling effect of the splendid costume jewellery worn by the rulers and courtiers of late eighteenth- and nineteenth-century Iran is epitomised in full-length portraits of 42 the ruler Fath Ali Shah (1797–1834), showing him elegant in long tight-waisted brocade robes. Personal ornaments include jewelled head-dresses and turbans in a variety of forms; bands with large gem-studded plaques worn on the upper arms, a fashion which lasted until about 1860; ropes of pearls worn as criss-crossed bandoliers; elaborate belts with ruby-studded buckles. Robes were adorned at neck and wrists with deep collars and cuffs stitched with pearls. Women's costume was equally lavish in its accessories – pearl- and ruby-studded caps, large ear-rings, necklaces of ropes of pearls, jewelled bands worn as collars and cuffs and also sewn to the hems of long full trousers and skirts.

While the Crown Jewels represent a sophisticated urban taste, jewellery of an equally striking parallel tradition was made and worn in the provinces of Iran. Here perhaps the most distinctive is that of the Türkmen tribal groups of north-east Iran and adjacent areas of Soviet Turkmenistan and north Afghanistan. Türkmen women, costumed in garments of sombre yet rich crimson and blue fabrics closely embroidered with geometrical motifs, were adorned with heavy cornelian-studded silver jewellery. Traditionally a woman acquired her jewellery through her family and at her wedding as part of her dowry. It was an indication of wealth and status in the community, but also had talismanic value. This

43 Tekke Türkmen women's jewellery, from Merv, Iran (19th century). The pieces include breast ornaments – a pair of *ẍ tumar*, a diamond-shaped *gönzuk* – and a *manlajlyk*, a married woman's headband. They are all made of flat plaques of gilded silver, inlaid with cornelians and adorned with chains and pendants.

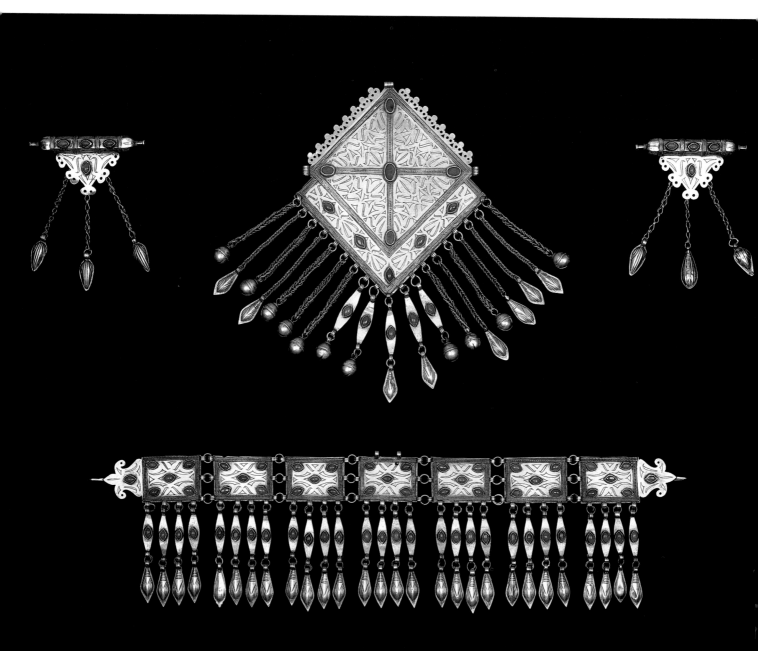

jewellery, which until recently could be obtained in the bazaars of Iran and Afghanistan, has been eagerly sought by collectors attracted by its striking massive forms. Pieces are now more easily found through western outlets.

The Türkmen jeweller was always fully employed and travelled between the camps of nomadic tribes or urban trading settlements. He worked within a narrow range of materials – silver, gold and some copper acquired as ingots or melted down from Russian, Afghan and Iranian coins, and the semi-precious stones of cornelian and, to a lesser extent, turquoise. Sheet silver was hammered into shape and inlaid with gilded silver in foliate and scroll motifs which contrasted with the chunky relief of cornelians and turquoises set in plain raised mounts. The techniques of drawing out silver wire, soldering and granulation were also employed.

While jewellery continues to be made today, the most handsome pieces may be dated to the late nineteenth and twentieth centuries. It was worn massed around the head, shoulders and arms, and some of the most ornate pieces are integral accessories to

44 Palestinian or Jordanian Bedouin women's bracelets (20th century): silver decorated in various techniques – repoussé, niello, and plaited and twisted wire.

head-dresses and hairstyles. Unmarried girls wore a comparatively simple head-dress consisting of an embroidered skull-cap covered with an ornament formed of a circular disc from which chains and pendants radiated. Married women had a more imposing head-dress in the form of a tall hat which was decorated across the front with a massive convex diadem or a more flexible band of linked plaques and chains. Various pendants adorned the hair, such as long multiple chains attached at the temples to frame the face, and heavy plaques joined to the end of the long plaits hanging down the wearer's back. Chains were also twisted into the hair. The neck and breast were lavishly adorned with choker bands and long chains, to which heavy triangular or diamond-shaped pendants were attached, sometimes functioning as amulet-cases. These pieces may be compared with the pendants depicted in miniature paintings of the sixteenth century, and possibly represent the survival of a form which had long gone out of fashion in urban jewellery. An especially distinctive ornament was a large circular cornelian-studded disc which functioned as a button fastening at the neck of a woman's robe. Wrists were encased in a pair of massive silver gauntlet-like bracelets which in form resembled the pearl-stitched cuffs of early nineteenth-century court dress. Contemporary Türkmen jewellery, while continuing in the traditional forms, is more limited in type and quality. It is often made of gilt metal stamped into the required shape and often inlaid with glass beads instead of cornelian and turquoise. The cap ornaments and temple pendants may be still seen on young girls, but increasingly jewellery is confined to the large circular neck fastening and hoop ear-rings.

In the Arab world no great royal collections comparable to those of Turkey and Iran have been preserved. City jewellery today shows an increasing uniformity, especially as the market in gold objects now relies much on imports from Italian workshops. To a certain extent, interesting jewellery may still be found, worn by the nomadic Bedouin peoples of Jordan and Syria, though increasingly the traditional silver is giving way to mass-produced gold objects purchased in the nearest city's shops and bazaars. As among the Türkmen of Iran, a woman's jewellery, which she began acquiring at the time of her marriage, was a fixed asset. It was valued as personal adornment, as a status symbol, as a financial investment and, in certain cases, as a protective talisman. Reflecting the

45 Bedouin girl from Jordan, mid-20th century. She wears a hair-slide made of four gold coins, and her gold nose-ring is decorated with filigree and granulation. She is also wearing necklaces made from glass and stone beads and cloves. Many beads are worn to protect against specific ailments.

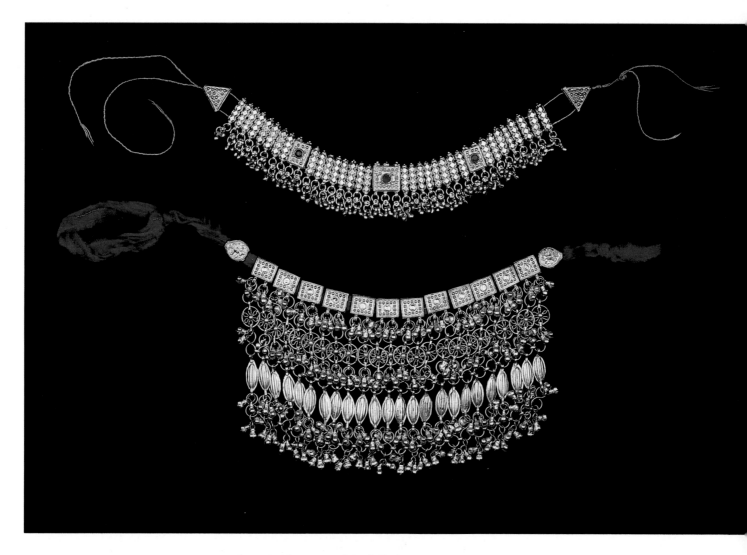

46 Girl's bridal jewellery from Yemen (20th century). Two elaborate silver necklaces consisting of hammered plaques, drawn filigree wire threaded with pellet beads and stamped pendants.

complex mixed nature of Arab Bedouin society, jewellery was made by silversmiths of, for example, Syrian, Armenian and Yemeni origin, who naturally introduced techniques and styles of their own regions. In general ornaments were made from sheet silver, decorated with engraving, repoussé, applied filigree wire, granulation and niello. The main concentration of jewellery was around a woman's neck, with chain necklaces set with pendants of various shapes, notably of stylised flowers, links and beads. Amulets of oval, rectangular, cylindrical and fish shape could be attached to the necklace. A choker consisting of a cotton band with a personal selection of silver ornaments and pendants could also be worn. Bead necklaces were made of coral and amber. Bracelets, always worn in pairs, were broad silver bands decorated with stylised designs in repoussé, niello or applied filigree. Plenty of finger-rings were worn, as silver bands either plain or set with stones. Nose-rings are found in hoop shape with crescent pendants ornamented with granulation and filigree motifs.

Two regions of the Arab Gulf illustrate different approaches to jewellery: Oman and Kuwait. Oman was always famed as a centre of the silversmith's craft, which was mainly based in the oasis town of Nizwa. While the traditional products are generally giving way to mass-produced gold items, examples of this distinctive craft can still be found. Silver was always worked from imported supplies, for example, the Maria Theresa dollar and, more recently, ingots from China. Old jewellery was also melted down and refashioned.

47 Woman's silver necklace from Oman (20th century), consisting of strings of tiny beads and amulet boxes with applied decoration.

Gold was used very sparingly as a means of providing a decorative ornamentation on silver. Techniques are comparable to those found in the Bedouin world. As with the Türkmen of Iran, pendant ornaments, here of circular shape with chains attached, are worn interwoven with the braids of hair hanging down the back. Ear-rings are in the form of hoops with pendant chains and plaques. The neck is hung with heavy chains or elaborate confections of silver beads to which square or rectangular amulet-boxes can be added. Wrists and ankles were encircled with massive chunky bands ornamented with engraved geometric designs or studded with rows of bosses. Finger-rings were made in pairs, one for each hand, consisting of deep bands with granulated ornament or pointed bezels. Toe-rings were simpler, consisting of bands with perhaps a single raised boss. Today women's jewellery fashions are changing. The traditional silver skull-cap of women from the southern province of Dhofar is now made exclusively in gold. It is also

48 Women's silver thumb- and finger-rings from Oman (20th century). The rings are decorated with chased designs and granulation.

49 Kuwaiti woman's wedding jewellery (mid-20th century). The heavy necklace is made of turquoise-studded sheet-gold plaques with repoussé and chased borders.

common practice for wealthy women in such towns as the capital Muscat to mix the jewellery of various regions for a fashionable effect at parties: in fact, using it in the manner of Western costume jewellery. For example, a woman will combine a gold head-dress from Dhofar with chains bought in the local bazaar and hand ornaments imported from India. One of the most striking forms of Omani jewellery is the silver dagger sheath still worn by men as a dress accessory. This is made of sheet silver elaborately decorated with chased and engraved scrolling foliage patterns and finely wrought geometric motifs interwoven in flat wire.

The jewellery of Kuwait presents an interesting blend of traditional Bedouin styles and foreign importations. Kuwait was basically a society in which desert Bedouin and settled town-dwellers, who made their living through trade and sea-faring, intermingled. Bedouin women who visited the outskirts of Kuwait when their tribes stopped there during their migration routes wore jewellery comparable to that of Syria and Jordan. This was of silver, and consisted of a profusion of necklaces, bracelets and finger-rings, often set with turquoise, coral and amber. Today these are increasingly replaced by gold purchased in the many jewellers' shopes of Kuwait City and its suburbs. Townswomen always preferred gold jewellery to silver and through the trading contracts of their families could add foreign pieces to their collections. Many pieces, for example, of Indian filigree goldwork set with rubies were imported.

Today, while shops sell imported, modern jewellery, traditional styles have survived. One of the most interesting survivals is the gold jewellery traditionally worn at weddings, which is usually made by Indian craftsmen resident in Kuwait. At its most lavish it consists of a set of head ornament, necklace, brooches, bracelets and rings. The head ornament, a circlet of linked gold plaques from which ribbon-like gold linked pendants hang at the back and sides of the wearer's head, compares to the example recovered from the ancient Sumerian city of Ur, and is remarkable evidence of the conservative survival of forms. Necklaces are heavy and ornate, extending to the wearer's waist and hung with plaques of leaf and crescent shape, often studded with pearls and turquoises. Bracelets and rings closely resemble the traditional styles worn in Syria and Jordan and Oman, but fashioned in gold and set with turquoise. The production also of such pieces in the Grand Bazaar in Istanbul provides a fitting concluding comment on both the complexity and vitality of Middle Eastern jewellery.

3

Asia

◆

INDIA

50 Son Koli fisherwoman from Bombay, richly adorned with the silver jewellery in which she has invested her surplus earnings. Her ornaments include ear-rings, two wire-wrapped torcs, a two-strand silver coin necklace, upper armlet and head ornaments.

n India the custom of wearing jewellery has an unbroken history reaching back 5,000 years into protohistoric times. No other nation in the world can challenge this impressive record, and India is unique in that even today, for various reasons, the use of jewellery continues with undiminished vitality.

India is ethnically complex, but all of its peoples possess distinctive styles of jewellery. The practice of adorning in this way is of considerable antiquity, although little ancient jewellery survives: cremation was the common funeral rite, so that grave finds of jewellery are rather rare. Archaeological discoveries from city, monastery and temple sites have provided us with some examples, but these alone are insufficient to give us a comprehensive idea of the development of traditional jewellery forms.

Detailed references to jewellery can be found in the enormous body of ancient Indian literature, including religious texts like the *Vedas*, the epics *The Mahabharata* and *The Ramayana*, and classic Sanskrit dramas of the fourth to fifth centuries AD, whose plots often emphasise the importance of jewellery. Visual evidence is fortunately provided by the huge quantity of jewellery accurately depicted on magnificent ancient stone and metal sculpture. These jewels, represented in painstakingly explicit detail, help to fill a significant part of the historic gap – especially in the so-called medieval period. Contemporary jewellery was often portrayed in the Mughal miniature paintings of the fifteenth to nineteenth centuries, and happily some similar pieces have survived destruction in the refiner's melting crucible.

By comparing the jewellery forms in current usage with those described, depicted or surviving from former times we find an astonishing number of archaic, prototypical forms still in use today. It can well be asked: what accounts for the continuity of ethnic jewellery in India? The answer is a complex one. Many factors contribute towards the preservation of traditional forms. The population of India is still essentially rural – over 70 per cent still live in villages, where local economy depends on cultivation. Rural people, and women in particular, tend to be conservative, with an active interest in preserving traditional designs in all aspects of the folk arts, and jewellery is no exception. The provincial silversmiths who make the silver jewellery for this market are fully aware of their customers' way of life, and no doubt through their work help to preserve traditional

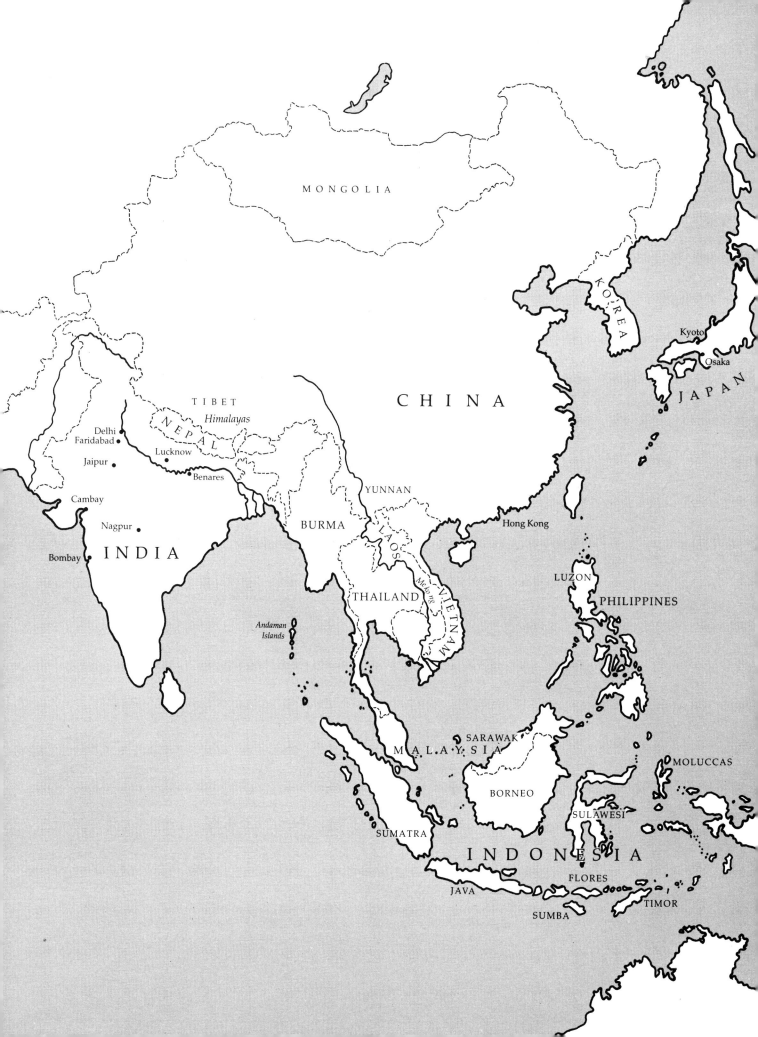

Map 2 India and the Far East, showing the principal place-names mentioned in the text.

forms. The active lifestyle of the average rural woman makes a robust approach to jewellery design necessary. In remote places unique forms evolved that have become identified with the particular groups who use them. Ancient archetypal designs also came to possess profound symbolic significance that today acts to ensure their preservation.

In contemporary societies jewellery may serve a number of functions. The same basic jewellery forms may be worn by all members of a particular community. Their designs are common knowledge and recognisable not only by all members of the group, but also by others outside the group. In one swift silent look an individual's group identity or even status within that group can be instantly identified. In such societies jewellery has become indispensable.

Jewellery is immediately associated with wealth, and great wealth is synonymous with social and political power. During the time of the Indian Mughal Dynasty (1526–1857), for example, jewellery was a major means by which central and provincial rulers proclaimed prestige, and was presented as gifts to ensure the loyalty of dependents of lower status whose lives revolved around the court. By maintaining a centralised store of wealth – which always included jewellery – the ruler made his position more secure. His power, reinforced and assured by his control of wealth and capital, would be demonstrated publicly at solemn state and religious functions, where sumptuary rules dictated the costumes and displays of jewellery worn by rulers and courtiers.

India has never produced sufficient indigenous gold or silver to satisfy national consumer demand. To fill this gap her merchants from time immemorial have insisted on payment in precious metals for Indian luxury products. Consequently India is today the world's largest repository of gold and silver, most of which was invested in jewellery to act as family insurance against the consequences of common disasters, such as drought, flood, famine, political upheaval and war. When the need arose jewellery could always be converted into currency, though the owner could only hope to receive the prevailing value of the weight of the precious metal in the object. Rural people commonly distrust the fluctuating value of currency and prefer to possess precious metal jewellery, which is reassuringly within reach, either on their person or in a safe hiding place. This accounts for the common sight of village women wearing silver jewellery even while working in the fields.

It would not be far from the truth to say that in traditional cultures practically all jewellery serves an amuletic function, some more obviously than others, even when the wearer may no longer be aware of its full significance. Religion plays an important role in Indian culture. Hinduism and Islam are widespread, but in remoter areas neither of them necessarily predominates. Hindu culture, however, is generally dominant, and has had great impact on all of India's inhabitants. Even though styles and usages in ornaments used by all exhibit inter-cultural influences, each group has evolved distinctive forms of jewellery which result specifically from their particular religious practice and way of life.

Every religious community in India (including converted Christians) uses amuletic jewellery. Its purpose is apotropaic – to work on behalf of the possessor by helping him or her to cope with natural forces that affect his or her life in a positive or negative manner. Prophylactic and homeopathic amulets offer protection against particular illnesses; others render the wearer immune to the effects of witchcraft, the chance of accident, threats from the environment or predatory animals. A special category of amulets counteracts the malignant influence of the ever-present evil eye, and is commonly placed on children, who are believed to be especially subject to malign influences.

While many amulets have negative powers of repulsion, others act to achieve a positive, beneficial purpose. Most common are those that act to ensure success in love, marriage, fertility and even in business transactions. A special type is the propitiatory Hindu amulet bearing a representation of a deity or several deities. Wearing this becomes an act of worship and a personal means of communicating with the Divine, whose protection is constantly solicited.

A great variety of materials is used for amulets in India. The oldest are natural substances found in the environment: parts of plants, birds and animals, cowrie shells and ammonites. Of special interest are naturally perforated, water-worn pebbles, which are believed to be inhabited by the goddess Lakshmi, and therefore particularly powerful and highly valued. All such substances produced by nature are believed already to possess power; in other cases power must be imbued in the material by a person specifically eligible to do so, such as a Hindu priest or an astrologer, following a

51 Jhoria-Muria boys from Bastar in Madhya Pradesh, wearing festive ornaments of cowrie shells, which are generally believed to ward off the effects of the evil eye.

prescribed ritual of consecration. Of the metals, gold and silver are especially favoured, for they are felt to be sacred and ritually pure, therefore already possessing beneficial powers. Coins of these metals are worn not simply as obvious forms of wealth, but as amulets to foster prosperity.

Amulets used by Hindus are quite distinct from those common in the Muslim communities. Many of their forms originated in a forgotten past, and can no longer be explained by wearers. A very common Hindu amulet type consists of a horizontal tubular container with attached loops, worn suspended by a cord or chain on the neck, arm or waist. They are never removed unless the support needs replacing. Among other magic objects, such a cylinder may contain a rolled-up piece of paper on which is written a protective Sanskrit sacred sentence or formula (*mantra*), or a diagrammatic charm (*yantra*).

52 Detail of a pendant amulet container on a silver necklace, from Jaisalmer, Rajasthan. It is partially gilded and set with coloured glass to imitate precious stones.

Particularly widespread are flat, sheet-metal amulets (*mandalia*), stamped or inscribed with magic inscriptions, occult symbols, or images of deities – usually the wearer's chosen deity (*ishta devata*), whom he elects to worship. Equally popular but more costly are the flattish, leaf-shaped, square or rectangular amulet containers which may also bear representations of deities, or have an opening at the front into which such a representation can be inserted. They may hold a variety of magic substances, depending on the amulet's function and the beliefs of the wearer. Another widely popular amulet commonly worn on the neck of children, but also by adults, is made with two tigers' claws, each mounted pointing outwards below an amulet box.

Amulets can be worn on any part of the body, but especially near the ears, nose, and the pudenda, to guard against the surreptitious entry of spirits through those bodily openings. They may also be placed at the temples, around the neck, on the upper arm, the wrist, chest, waist, ankles and toes. No single amulet can ever offer total protection from all dangers, though some are shields against more than one, which explains why some people wear several amulets simultaneously. Amulets can be elaborately decorated and at times their embellishment reaches an astonishing richness that transforms them into highly ornamental jewels.

India's Muslim community (about 10 per cent of the population) uses distinctive forms of jewellery. Although influenced by Hindu prototypes, these employ symbols used only by Muslims, such as the crescent moon and star. One characteristic of Muslim charms is their common use of calligraphic inscriptions in Arabic letters: figural depiction is forbidden by the Qur'ān.

53 Bhil man from Rajasthan. He is wearing a necklace with three tubular amulet-cases and another with four *phul deota* plaques, three stamped with the name of a deity, and the fourth depicting a deity riding a horse.

54 White jade plaque amulet (*haldili*) from Delhi, a type worn by Muslims. The front is set *kundan*-style with diamonds and carved foiled stones in a design of birds, stars, a crescent moon and a flowering plant. The reverse, worn in contact with the body, is engraved with a passage from the Qur'ān.

The most common Muslim amulet form, often worn by children, is a container designed to hold an inscription on paper or parchment, usually a short invocation (*sutra*) from the Qur'ān, which is commonly believed to offer potent protection against the various evils that can befall humans. These inscriptions, usually written in graceful cursive scripts, can be decidedly decorative. When visible on the amulet's exterior, the characters are ingeniously arranged for reasons of harmonious balance to fill the area.

More permanent than paper are the amulets made of tablet- or shield-shaped slabs of various hardstones – especially agate, bloodstone, cornelian, crystal, lapis lazuli and jade. All these stones are believed to possess special prophylactic qualities, but jade (nephrite), introduced to India from China via Central Asia in Mughal times, is considered most efficacious. Its popularity rests in the belief that, when worn in contact with the body, jade can control heart palpitations, divert lightning, and resist the action of poisons.

Some hardstone amulets have inscriptions engraved on both sides. Others have an inscription on the reverse which is worn next to the skin, and often have a floral design symbolising the tree of life on the obverse, visible side, embellished with inlays of gold and precious stones. Carving is done by a specialist lapidary, and because of the high cost of these items, they are usually purchased by the wealthy, who frequently have them set in elaborate precious metal mounts.

Other symbols used on Muslim amulets include cabalistic or magic squares with rows of three or more compartments, each containing ciphers or letters believed to emanate mystic powers. Typical are numbers so arranged that their total in each column in any direction equals the same mystic number; or palindromic word squares whose letters when similarly read spell out the same magic word. Believed to possess great power, this type of charm has its equivalents among Hindus and other groups.

In all Indian communities, but especially among male Hindus, the progress of the individual from birth to death in rite-of-passage events is marked by purification ceremonies, where jewellery may play an important role. For example, at birth a ceremony is performed during which a protective gold or silver amulet on a black cord is attached to the child's right wrist, neck or waist to protect it during the specially vulnerable period of its first days. At the name-giving ritual, performed twelve days after birth, a stud or small ring is inserted into the child's ear, and sometimes nose, to act as a protective amulet. Children are believed to be especially vulnerable to malignant spirits, and such ornaments are believed to engage the spirit's attention and divert it from the child itself. In another custom that presumes the gullibility of evil spirits, boys are made to wear a small nose-ring, typically a girl's ornament. The intention is to dupe the spirit into believing the wearer to be a girl and therefore, in local idiom, a less valuable subject of interest.

At puberty girls theoretically become eligible for marriage, and to make them more appealing parents often bedeck them with many ornaments. Marriage is probably the most significant event of a person's life. Marriage customs vary greatly across this vast country, and in today's changing social and economic climate they are undergoing rapid change. The following account can, therefore, only be of a general nature.

Marriages in India are for the most part still arranged by parents on their child's behalf, and a woman's dowry is negotiated between the fathers of the couple. A normal rural dowry, carried in procession to the groom's house, includes clothing, household articles, and – very importantly – an agreed amount of precious metal jewellery. Its type, number and value (usually referred to in terms of total weight) is determined by local social traditions, and the economic circumstances of the families involved.

The jewellery and other objects a bride is given under the terms of the marriage agreement is her main form of property (*stridana*), and wealth in the form of jewellery is often her only exclusive possession. At the wedding ceremony the bride is lavishly clothed and bedecked with as much jewellery as her resources will allow. After the ceremony, when a rural bride finally goes to live in her new husband's home, she will load herself with much – if not all – of the jewellery she possesses. At this time her appearance is crucial, particularly in the eyes of her new female relatives, as it may determine basic attitudes they adopt towards her that can influence her entire future in that household. Normally a bride will not remove her jewellery for several months, or the whole first year, even when bathing and sleeping, as to do so is considered bad luck.

Some form of marriage ornament is indispensable for every married Indian woman, to proclaim her marital status in her community. The ornaments mentioned here which

56 Silver marriage pendant (*thali*) from Tamil Nadu. This form is one of many variants of this ornament widely worn in south India.

serve this purpose are used by Hindus and related communities, but Muslim women have been influenced by similar ideas and have their equivalents. The overall picture is complicated by the fact that each of the basic types can be found in a considerable diversity of forms, and variants of them are current in different places.

In general in almost all of southern India, including Maharashtra, Karnatika, Andhra Pradesh, Kerala and Tamil Nadu, marriage ornaments are worn on the neck. The most common is a gold pendant (*thali*), whose form varies from community to community. Consecrated when it is tied on a wife's neck by her husband during the marriage ceremony, it is only removed when the cord needs replacing or when the woman becomes a widow. Other talismans may be worn on the same cord. Particularly popular in Maharashtra, Karnatika and Andhra Pradesh is the *mangalsutram* ('auspicious cord'), and its popularity is gaining elsewhere. It consists of a pure gold *thali* pendant, simple or elaborate according to taste and means, suspended on the chest by one or two strands of small black glass beads.

Among rural women in northern India head ornaments are commonly used to indicate marriage. Very common is the *tikli* type, which again has many variants. It is worn on the forehead at the base of the central parting of the hair, to which it may be attached. Alternatively, it may be held on the head by one or more cords, or even elaborate chains. Of gold or silver, its form can be flat and circular, ball-like, or conical. The visible side can be relatively simple or elaborately ornamented, in some cases even paved with diamonds.

In Himachal Pradesh an extreme form of head ornament is the large dome-shaped

⁵⁷ silver or gold *chak*, worn on the crown of the head. Some have smaller flanking side *chaks*, attached to the main one with chains. Another interesting ornament (*jhumar*), worn by Muslim women on the side of the head, generally but not always as an indication of marriage, consists of a series of chains or strings of beads or pearls, spreading out from an ornamental spacer and attached by hooks to the hair.

Nose ornaments are also commonly worn as marriage ornaments, especially in northern India, and various kinds are worn throughout the sub-continent. Nose ornaments only appeared in India around the end of the sixteenth century, and are believed to have been introduced by the Mughals: their earliest depiction is in Mughal and Rajput miniature paintings. The most common type is the stud (*phul*), worn through a hole in the

57 Gaddi woman from Mandi, in Himachal Pradesh. She wears a silver marriage ornament (*chak*) on the top of her head. Her ear-rings are attached by chains to hair-clips and ornamented with bells, and she has a triple-strand necklace of silver beads.

58 Woman from Tatiana, District Sirmur, Himachal Pradesh. She wears a silver nose-ring (*nath*) whose weight is supported by chains and hooks attached to the head covering and the ornament at the back of the head. Her silver choker is composed of many elements threaded and joined to triangular end-spacers. Her jewellery is variously decorated with granulation, stamping and wrapped wire.

left ala and secured by a screw fitting inside the nostril, or by a hook. Its size varies from a small gold ball or diamond to a large flat disc with a highly ornamented surface. Additionally, the stud may have small attachments like a fringe of hanging chains or small pendants. In some places stud-type nose ornaments are worn simultaneously in both left and right alae.

Large nose-rings (*nath*) are also worn in the left ala. They may be plain silver or gold hoops, but they may also be extravagantly ornamented with enamel, pearls and precious 58 stones. Heavy nose-rings must be supported by cords or chains hooked to the hair or head covering to hold the ornament flat against the cheek, otherwise their weight would distort the nose. The third basic type of nose ornament, usually of gold, is a pendant 59 (*bulak*) hung from a hole in the septum. Simple rings are known, but some pendants may

59 Silver nose-ring (*bulak*) from Mandi, Himachal Pradesh, decorated with granulation and set with turquoises. It covers the mouth and must be lifted when eating.

be so large and complex that they hang over the mouth, and must be lifted up when eating. To persons outside this culture nose ornaments are probably the strangest of all Indian jewellery, although in context they are attractive and meaningful.

Other ornaments may be associated with marriage, although they are normally not involved in the ceremony itself. Throughout India anklets, worn in pairs, one on each ankle, are common, though not all function as marriage ornaments. Rigid anklets may be made in one or two parts, the latter hinged or fastened together by pins or rivets. Flexible anklets usually consist of a chain or system of chains, or wide bands composed of small interlinked elements. Among the poorer people and especially among more isolated communities it is common to find anklets of base metals like white metal, copper, and copper alloys, such as brass and bronze. These metals have little intrinsic value, and

60 Pair of hollow silver anklets from Sambalpur, Orissa. They are constructed in two parts held together by rosette-headed side screws, and ornamented with granulation, applied lozenge-shaped units and wrapped beaded wire.

extremely archaic, elaborate forms have survived and are still made. In most places anklets are of silver; the use of gold is avoided, as the wearing of gold on the feet has always been considered to be demeaning to that sacred metal.

Toe-rings, also relative late-comers, are now worn all over India, where many people go barefoot. In the north especially they are associated with marriage. The subjects depicted on them may have symbolic significance, such as the fish, fertility, and the scorpion, which acts as an apotropaic, protective amulet.

Wrist ornaments of various kinds may be worn by married women, especially bangles, which in India universally have this function. Gold is especially favoured, but is less common than other materials. Lac bangles, made of the resin secreted by the female insect *Tachardia lacca*, are especially ancient in usage. They are worn singly or in sets of graduated size, and made in many colours and with many forms of surface decoration, including tiny mirrors and gold leaf. Iron bangles are sometimes encased in gold, and

61 Woman from Pali, Rajasthan. The ivory bangles on her upper arm and wrist were originally dyed a deep auspicious red, now worn to pink. They are believed to ease childbirth. She also wears a silver necklace of square plaques and a wire-wrapped torc of an ancient type.

those of conch shell are traditionally worn by married women in West Bengal. In Rajasthan ivory bangles are common, often dyed an auspicious red. In some places they are worn in sets that go from wrist to armpit. Because of its high cost and increasing non-availability, ivory is being replaced by white plastic.

Glass bangles are the most common of all. The largest centre for their manufacture is probably Faridabad in Uttar Pradesh, where they are produced in infinite variety by the million. Every town of any size, and certainly every city, has a special bangle bazaar, where women spend hours making careful deliberations about their selection of patterns and colours. In remoter parts of India, where no bangle bazaars exist, itinerant bangle sellers ply their trade. When a woman has made her selection, always in the smallest possible size to reduce the chance of breakage, the dealer must place the bangles on her wrists. Crouching on the ground before the dealer, she winces in pain as he slowly squeezes her purchases over her compressed, lubricated hands. Glass bangles are in any

62 Woman from Kinnaur, Himachal Pradesh, adorned with necklaces of coral and turquoises, silver head ornaments with cascades of small silver leaves, and a shawl clasp. The people of this Himalayan area wear a profusion of jewellery over their heavy woollen clothing; the forms of some of their ornaments are influenced by those worn in nearby Tibet.

case fragile, and when broken must be replaced, and the process again endured. By universal custom, when a married woman becomes a widow, as an expression of grief on losing her husband and entering that sad social status of widowhood, she smashes her bangles and removes all other ornaments she normally wears.

57   The use of bells and balls on many forms of jewellery is typically Indian. The jingling sound they make when the wearer moves has a decided erotic appeal to Indian men, as witnessed by many literary references. The origin of their use, it has been claimed, is the practice of purdah (parda, 'curtain'), a custom among Muslims but also among some Hindus in which married women are secluded from public sight and from men not related to them by blood or marriage. In families where the purdah system is in effect the jingling warns men of a woman's presence or approach. In some cases other functions have been suggested for jewellery which produces sounds. For example, the tinkling of metal fragments or pebbles placed inside hollow anklets during manufacture, or of bells

attached to toe-rings is calculated to frighten away scorpions and snakes, not to mention evil spirits. Undeniably, sound adds another dimension to the charm of traditional Indian ornaments.

Many other purely decorative types of jewellery also exist, although these too may serve other functions. India's rich jewellery tradition has developed to include its use on every part of the body that can possibly support it. A reason often advanced to explain this practice is the tropical climate of most of the country which makes the need for clothing minimal and leaves parts of the body exposed, and therefore available for ornamentation. But even in the cold Himalayan region women wear a profusion of
62 ornaments over their heavy woollen clothing. One must conclude that climate is not a dominating factor in the case.

In general rural women arrange their jewellery symmetrically on each side of the body, the ornaments in equal numbers and if possible matching in design. In many cases communities decree a specific sequence for these ornaments and every woman strives to achieve the established number and types. On the hands and arms are worn armlets, bracelets and finger-rings. Armlets that often resemble bracelets but are much larger are
9 worn above the elbow. They are an ancient form which, though still in use today, seems to be declining in popularity. Rigid armlet types may be made from sheet metal to make flat or hollow, tubular annular forms, with or without an opening. Wire of any gauge can be wound in loops or spirals, wrapped around a core, or plaited. A special type, known as *vanki* in Tamil Nadu, consists of two heavy, continuous v-shaped sections of wire joined together; this form allows the armlet to be adjusted easily to accommodate any upper arm size. A single flat or curved rigid element – either of sheet metal or cast – is bound to the arm by two cords.

The basic flexible armlet type is the *bajuband*, which consists of three elements hinged
159 together and held on the arm by cords or chains. A second flexible type is made of many narrow elements, whose vertical edges have a variety of angular contours that fit alongside each other like a jigsaw puzzle. These are held together by cords which either pass through the body of each hollow element, or through loops attached at their top and bottom. Armlets may be decorated with a variety of metalworking techniques, and the more elaborate employ enamel and precious stones. They may have attached metal or stone pendants, or decorative yarn tassels, some of them reaching extraordinary lengths.

Wrist ornaments exist in enormous variety all over India. Rigid penannular bracelets of circular or ovoid form, which are cast or forged with animal-head terminals, are an extremely archaic type. Unlike bangles, they have an opening to facilitate putting them on and taking them off. Bracelets made of a flat metal band can vary in width from narrow
166 to very broad, cuff-like forms. Other rigid bracelet types may be made in two parts hinged together, and employ various kinds of fastenings, such as screws or movable pins. Flexible bracelets can be made from wire, woven, braided or intermeshed. Another distinct flexible type is made up of one or several strands of small units strung together on a thick cord which passes through the loops attached to each unit.

Finger-rings are worn on all fingers, including the thumbs. There are many types, made of various materials. The innumerable forms of metal rings can broadly be divided into those with and those without a bezel (the part of a ring meant to hold a decorated device, seal or stone). Rings set with personal seals are less common today than formerly,
63 but rings set with stones are ubiquitous. The particular stone may be chosen for reasons other than mere attractiveness. According to Hindu astrology, each of the nine planets in the Hindu universe is represented by a specific stone. Every Indian knows the planet dominant at the time of his or her birth, as it is believed to exert a strong influence on that person's life. By wearing the stone associated with the planet, its effect can be enhanced

63 *Right* Group of gold rings from North India, dating to the 18th century and richly set with a range of stones: rubies and a sapphire (*top left*), rubies and a pearl (*top right*), and (*bottom*) eleven different precious and semi-precious stones.

64 *Below* Multi-unit, interlinked gold hand ornament (*ratan phul*) from Bombay, set with diamonds and rubies. This compound type of ornament is worn by brides: in towns they are made of gold and in rural areas of silver.

or mitigated, according to whether the planet is malign or benign. A very popular arrangement of stones, called *nava ratna* ('nine stones'), is used in rings and other kinds of ornaments, each representing one of the planets. By wearing an ornament with the *nava ratna* stones the wearer is provided with universal protection.

In a special category is the large thumb-ring set with a circular mirror. A rural bride wearing such a ring during her marriage ceremony, her eyes cast down as modesty demands, can see in it a reflection of her husband's face, sometimes for the first time. Another type of thumb-ring, now obsolete, is the archer's ring of jade or gold, at times set with gems and embellished with enamel. Its Central Asian origin accounts for its popularity among high-ranking men during Mughal times.

Braid ornaments constitute a special class of jewellery, very 'Indian' in character. One of the glories of Indian women is their lustrous long black hair, which has always had an erotic appeal for their menfolk. Most women part their hair in the centre, hence the symmetrical design of several head ornaments and the customs among married women of placing red powder at the parting. The rest of the hair may be coiled into a bun, decorated by a range of ornaments, such as large round plaques and hairpins of many kinds, some with attached dangling chains and bells.

Perhaps more common is the custom of plaiting the hair into a long braid that hangs at the back. The braid is often thickened with either additional hair or skeins of black thread, both ending with tassels of yarn or metal and fringed with bells or balls. An elaborate braid ornament especially popular among south Indian Bharatanatyam dancers repre-
65 sents a multi-headed stylised cobra: Shesha, the primeval serpent. The head, its largest

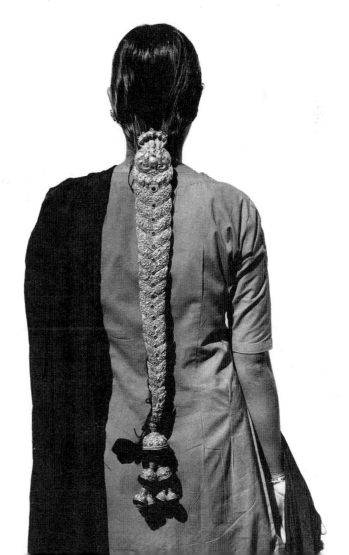

65 Gold-plated silver braid ornament worn by a woman from Hyderabad, Andhra Pradesh. The articulated ornament takes the form of the serpent Sesha; at the end is a cluster of bells (*paranda*).

66 *Above* Two pairs of gold
ear-rings (*karan phul*) from Jaipur
in Rajasthan, set *kundan*-style with
diamonds and rubies, enriched
with enamel and with pendants of
pearls.

part, is fixed at the top of the braid, and the stylised body descends in articulated
segments over the rest of its length.

Ear ornaments are worn through holes pierced in any of the external parts of the ear.
Piercing is the only indigenous Indian system to hold ear ornaments. Studs can be
attached to any part of the ear, but especially the helix, tragus and lobe; the shank passes
through the ear and is held in place by a simple or ornamental screw or pressure fitting.
Rings small or large are worn through a single hole in the lobe. Multiple rings worn in
series are each placed in a separate hole in the helix. Pendants can be suspended from a
loop or ring, or form an addition to an ear-stud placed in the lobe.

The forms and sizes of ear ornaments vary enormously. They can be decorated in an
immense number of ways, including embellishments with enamel, stones or pearls.
Almost any type can have additional small decorative chains and hanging miniature
pendants, often in small leaf shapes, balls or bells. Some ear-rings are so heavy they must
be supported by a cord or chain, often elaborate, that passes over the ear or is hooked to
the hair. Other types of unsupported heavy ear ornaments are worn from a hole in the
lobe, which as a result is permanently stretched to an unimaginable degree. The large
disc plugs used in Gujarat, and the various kinds of heavy ear-ring worn by some people
in Tamil Nadu are examples.

Of the basic types of jewellery not yet discussed the most important is the necklace.
Necklaces have always been especially popular because they are worn as an adjunct to
the face and contribute much to concepts of facial beauty. They are found in a staggering
assortment of forms, styles and materials. The most ephemeral, and arguably the earliest
to be devised by man, is the ubiquitous Indian garland. Commonly worn by brides and
grooms, garlands are also presented to honour a guest or important person, and used for

67 *Opposite* Street vendor's display
of beads and rosaries, spread on
the ground before the entrance to
the Jaganath Temple at Puri,
Orissa. The materials used are
seeds (large brown *rudrakshas*),
basil stems (*tulsi*), clear and
coloured glass, and hardstones.

religious purposes, such as decorating and venerating the image of a deity. Favourite garland flowers are jasmine, rose and marigold.

Bead necklaces have always held a great fascination for all people in India, and indeed elsewhere. Ancient beads have been found at many archaeological sites in India, and it is presumed that originally they all had amuletic purposes. The materials used for beads exploit the resources of the vegetable, animal and mineral worlds, and the manner of
67 their use is infinite. Important because of its religious associations is the basil plant (*Ocimum sanctum*), sacred to Vishnu and widely cultivated by Hindus for ceremonial purposes. Its stems are dried and cut into sections that are strung as beads. Spices such as cloves and cardamom seeds are used to make aromatic necklaces and garlands, the latter a speciality of Tanjore, Tamil Nadu. From the animal world, bone, horn, ivory, coral and pearls have all been used for beads. Cowrie shells, also used in necklaces, have found their way by trade from their source in the Maldive and Laccadive Islands to the most remote areas of India. Among the minerals most commonly used for beads of all sizes, forms and colours is glass. Manufactured at centres like Papanaidupetta in Andhra Pradesh, Indian beads today replace the great quantities of glass beads formerly imported from the famous production centres of Europe, such as Venice and Jablonz in Czechoslovakia.

The abundance of locally available hardstones – agate, bloodstone, cornelian, chalcedony, garnet and others – long ago led to a flourishing bead-making industry in the city of Cambay on the Arabian Sea coast. Besides satisfying Indian demand, this centre provided the ancient world with its magnificent products, and the industry continues today. Still using the laborious hand techniques of cutting, shaping, polishing and drilling, thousands are here employed making beads of all sizes and forms. As well as being strung into a variety of decorative necklaces and rosaries, the beads are sold in bulk by weight.

Beads are also made from all metals, but especially silver and gold. Gold beads commonly fabricated from thin-gauge metal are filled with lac to support them and prevent the metal from becoming dented in use, a practice also used for other hollow gold ornaments. The manner of combining beads and the ways of stringing them are endless. They can be used alone in a necklace; as spacers between units of other forms and materials; and they can be strung in strands to support a central pendant or locket which often serves as a charm container.

The most ancient type of metal necklace is probably the rigid torc (*hansuli*), still widely
155 worn in India and found in many variants. In its most basic form it is a solid curved bar, forged from a single precious metal ingot. The front is often square or rectangular in section, and the back round, generally tapering to two curved ends which are forced apart to place the torc on the neck. Surfaces are commonly decorated by carving, chasing and stamping.

Flexible necklaces are made from a series of elements strung on a chain or cord, perhaps with a larger central ornament or pendant. Long necklaces (*mala*), their elements either strung closely together or spaced on cords or chains, can reach to the navel; they are related in concept to the garland, which in India is always very long. Almost universal
69 in India is the *champakali* necklace with elements designed after the venerated fragrant yellow flower bud of the *champa* tree (*Michelia champaca*). Many other traditional designs of necklace elements are based on bud and flower forms, or other natural objects often considered to be sacred by Hindus. An example is the large pendant or locket in the form of a hanging leaf of the pipal tree (*Ficus religiosa*), sacred to Vishnu.

Flexible belts of silver, gold or other metals are worn tightly around the waist to help create the ideal small waistline considered so attractive in an Indian woman. Others are

68 Silver necklace from Jaipur, Rajasthan. The pendants, strung on a black cord, are die-stamped, each in the form of a pair of stylised tigers' claws, a popular Hindu amulet.

designed to rest loosely on the hips in the same manner as the *mekhala* belts abundantly represented on ancient sculptures. Handmade chains, commonly used for belts, are often technically remarkable. One such is the tightly braided, snake-like type, made to appear smooth by being pulled through a drawplate, which by compressing and smoothing the surface also makes it more supple. Belts made of this kind of chain are classically worn by rural men in Gujarat, Rajasthan, Maharashtra and Madhya Pradesh. Threaded over them are various kinds of ornaments: in Kerala looped amulets are used in this way. A remarkable type of heavy chain, whose links could be more than an inch in section, was formerly used by Koli fishermen in the Bombay area. Rigid belts, adjustable by a series of spaced holes at one end, are made of spring hardened sheet silver, so they retain their form. Their surfaces are decorated in various ways, including the attachment of bunches of small balls. Precious metal belts require a relatively large amount of metal and they are costly, so they are now slowly becoming obsolete.

Jewellery continues to be made in India today in the manner practised for millennia, with each step in the production carried out by a craftsman specialising in one of the various techniques of manufacture and decoration. As a typical case, an enamelled gold object set with stones requires the work of at least six artisans: the goldsmith, who fashions the object into its basic form without surface decoration; an embosser, chaser or engraver, who decorates the object and prepares it for enamelling; the enameller; the stone-setter, possibly a specialist diamond-setter; and the polisher, who hand-burnishes any exposed metal areas. Other related specialists include the lapidary, the stone-dealer, and the gold-foil beater.

Ancient types of hand-tool and traditional production methods are still normally used for manufacturing jewellery, although in the big cities some machines, such as polishing lathes and rolling mills, have now been introduced. The basic techniques of jewellery-making are described elsewhere in this book, but a few processes deserve to be singled out for mention here because they contribute largely to the character of much Indian jewellery.

In India jewellery is often made by assembling pre-fabricated elements. Die-stamping of sheet metal is a common way of quickly and easily making any number of positive repeats of a negative pattern engraved in the die. Small decorative die-stamped units, such as flowers, are commonly used to cover the junctions of border wires and other joins. Examples of larger-scale stampings are the *champa*-bud forms of the *champakali* necklace, and *mandalia*, with their images of deities.

Enamelling has also long been practised by Indian jewellers. In gold Mughal-style gem-set jewellery enamel is sometimes used on the front, generally in areas of solid colour contrasting with the stones. Characteristic of this type of jewellery, however, are the intricate, small-scale designs enamelled on the backs, where they remain unseen. Perhaps part of the explanation for this practice may be the artisan's delight in his own craft, but probably more important are the requirements of technology. The 22-carat gold used by Indian jewellers is very soft and subject to abrasion. Enamelling the back of an object, where it is in contact with the skin, reduces abrasion and loss of metal. In addition, the enamel itself helps to lend rigidity to objects made of thin sheet gold.

The main type of enamelling practised in India is champlevé. Today there are three major enamelling centres in India, each with its own distinctive traditional style of work: Jaipur (Rajasthan), Benares (Uttar Pradesh) and Lucknow (Uttar Pradesh). Jaipur enamel on gold is considered to be outstanding. Here the tradition of Mughal styles of work is perpetuated, and some of the finest enamel work being executed today is comparable in every way with the best found on Mughal jewellery. Jaipur enamels are justly famous for the clear brilliant red they call pigeon's blood. Not accidentally, the Jaipuri enamel palette includes transparent colours that correspond to the most important coloured stones: red (corresponding with ruby), green (emerald), blue (sapphire). Opaque colours are also used, especially white and turquoise. The use of particular colours in a design has led to established styles of enamel work, designated according to the ground colour used: transparent red, transparent blue, transparent green, opaque blue, opaque white, and opaque white outline. To increase the reflection of light through the transparent enamels and thus enhance their colour brilliance, the areas to be enamelled are engraved with parallel lines, which also improves the bonding between the enamel and metal.

Benares enamel, once applied only to gold, is often referred to as 'pink enamel'. Its name comes from a style of decoration in which relatively large dominant areas of opaque white are overpainted with pink floral motifs, such as the rose or lotus. Blue is also used in the same manner, although less commonly. An outline of the design is painted on the opaque white area with very finely ground red enamel. While these lines are wet the colour is teased out with a small brush to create a gradually fading pink. This shaded effect is only possible on an opaque white ground, so the same result is achieved in Benares today on silver objects.

Lucknow enamel is also done in the champlevé style, but on silver. It employs a dominant transparent green and blue palette. The transparent red used on gold, when applied to silver, appears an orange-brown, which accounts for the occasional appearance of this colour on silver Lucknow objects: the colour-balanced red required for use on silver is not available in India. Lucknow enamelling was mainly used on objects such as small boxes and *hukka* bases, and it is less common on jewellery.

69 Silver necklace (*champakali*) from Delhi. The stylised pendant elements strung on black cord represent the fragrant flower buds of the *champa* tree, and are set with foil-backed, cabochon-cut glass 'stones', imitating diamonds.

70, 71 *Left* Gold enamelled necklace from Jaipur, Rajasthan. The front (70, *top*) is ornamented with a green enamel ground set with diamonds, rubies and pendant pearls. The reverse (71, *below*), never seen, is enamelled with minutely scaled designs of flowers and birds.

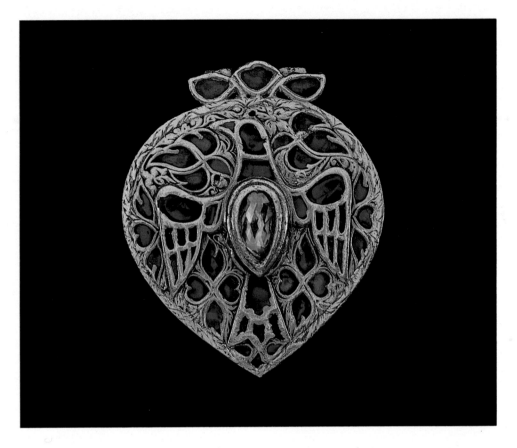

72 *Right* Mughal-style gold pendant of the 17th century. The front depicts a splayed eagle against a floral ground, inlaid with rubies, emeralds and a central faceted diamond. The reverse bears a champlevé-enamel parrot amid flowers.

As well as in these three main centres, some good enamel work is still produced in Delhi and Nathdwara (Rajasthan). Delhi enamelling in the past was equal in quality to that of Jaipur. Work produced there today is similar in style to Jaipur enamelling, although executed more often on silver. Nathdwara enamelling is of a more commercial type, done in transparent colours on silver. Beads and plaques used as pendants are the major products.

A form of gem-setting characteristic of Mughal-style jewellery is carried out by a traditional method closely associated with India. This closed-setting technique is probably about four hundred years old and may have come from Persia. The stones commonly used in traditional Mughal-style jewellery are generally irregular in outline and asymmetrically faceted (cap cut). Kundan work (*kundan*, 'pure gold'), using a very soft foil of about 23-carat gold, is a method devised to simplify the setting of these irregularly contoured stones. After all other decorative processes are completed, the stone is set in place in the lac-filled hollow unit of the object, over a piece of metallic foil. The purpose of the foil is to reflect light entering the stone from the front – the only way possible in a traditional closed setting – back through the stone to the viewer. For diamonds or colourless zircons (used to simulate diamonds) the foil is of silver or pure tin, which never oxidises. Tin foil also backs glass polished to simulate stones, commonly used in rural jewellery. For coloured stones the upper surface of the foil is pre-coated with a thinly applied layer of a transparent lac to which an appropriately coloured pigment has been added to enhance the colour of the stone: blue for sapphire, red for ruby, green for emerald.

Once the stone is in position the setter, using a steel stylus, leads and guides a folded strip of kundan gold foil around the stone. With variously shaped tool ends he forces the gold into the space between the setting and the stone, modelling the foil so that it slightly

73 Angami Naga man, whose primitive ornaments exploit natural materials, such as the tucan feathers in his head-dress, the blue wings of the Indian Roller (*Coracacias benghalensis*) in the ear pendants, as well as cowrie shells, beads and yarn for the necklaces.

overlaps the stone edge. As gold of this high purity can be self-welded when cold, the gold becomes solid and forms a ridge around the stone that holds it in place.

Because traditional jewellery still plays great importance in the life of most Indian people, it is still possible to find jewellery with a high degree of workmanship. Skill is recognised and appreciated by the public, even when they may not be able to afford to possess such an object or fully understand the technologies involved. The more evident the skill of its construction and decoration, the more prestigious the jewellery. Appreciation of this kind can have the effect of pushing the jeweller towards realising a higher standard of achievement, aiming at minuteness of scale and detail in the surface ornament, which comes to characterise this work. A common example, mentioned above, is the elaborate decoration of parts of an object which are never seen, such as the enamelled backs of Mughal-style jewellery, still made today.

The study of the development of jewellery in India is an exploration of an *al fresco*, living museum. Across this huge sub-continent can be found the entire range of personal ornament, from the primitive adornments employing materials provided by nature, to the most sophisticated achievements of the goldsmith's art in dazzling ornaments made of precious metals and stones.

Today, as business interests exploit any possible area of gain, relatively large factories exist in towns producing silver jewellery for rural people, and large markets can be found in every major city to which rural people come to purchase silver jewellery. Urban jewellers also work for a more sophisticated clientele who until recently would not consider wearing silver ornaments because of their rural associations. Those living in towns have always shown a decided preference for gold jewellery, which, because of the high cost of the metal (higher in India than elsewhere in the world), developed characteristic light-weight, delicate forms entirely different from the robust silver rural jewellery. Although the distinction between rural and urban jewellery is clear, an interesting area of overlap exists. Some rural people consider all things emanating from the towns to be superior and are influenced by urban fashions, so designs intended for gold jewellery may be interpreted in lowly silver. Conversely, traditional rural designs may be 'urbanised' by the use of gold and precious stones. Such objects are commissioned by those wealthy enough to afford them because, though affluent, these people still wish to be identified culturally with their rural community.

Fashions change more rapidly in towns and urban goldsmiths tend to be more open to foreign ideas, so that a whole additional range of international-style jewellery also exists in India. However, when custom or preference dictate, particularly when selecting jewellery for a daughter's dowry, an Indian family is still able to draw upon a vast reservoir of traditional styles that continue to be made and worn today.

THE FAR EAST

♦

74 Lisu women from the Golden Triangle, bedecked in jewellery for their New Year festivities. Their costumes are covered with silver dangles, buttons and buckles; their ear-rings are linked by metal chains that pass under the chin.

The Far East is a vast geographical zone, ranging from the cool steppe lands of the north to the humid rainforests of the tropical south. It is bounded in the west by the great plateau of Tibet, which lies before the Himalayas, and in the east by the wide expanse of the Pacific. The region comprises nations such as China, the world's most populous state, and Japan, the second largest industrial power, as well as important developing countries like Indonesia. The jewellery traditions of the Far East reflect this immense environmental, cultural and economic diversity.

Archaeological research has revealed an ancient heritage. Perforated beads excavated at Zhoukoudian in China show that personal ornaments were used by Paleolithic hunter-gatherers, and by the Neolithic period the sophisticated art of jade-carving was known in what is now Zhejiang Province (*c.* 5000 BC). Finely polished pendants and beads were being produced in south-east China during the third millennium BC.

Ancient forms of jewellery are not only limited to China and significant discoveries have been made in South-East Asia and Japan. The Ban Chiang excavations in Thailand, one of the oldest Neolithic sites in Asia, have yielded jewellery, as have the Ban Kao burials and settlements (*c.* 1700 BC), where polished bracelets and beads have been uncovered. Fragments of what may have been an ornamental comb have been found in Japan (*c.* 1000 BC), as well as pendants made of pottery, shell and stone that were used by the hunter-fishers of the ancient Jómon culture.

Given the diversity of ethnic groups, their varied historical circumstances and the sheer size of the region, it is not surprising that numerous different kinds of ornamentation should have evolved over time. While the contemporary forms of jewellery are characterised by their immense diversity, rather than any single interlinking theme, it is clear that these distinctive traditions did not develop in complete isolation, and interaction between the emerging societies has been an important vehicle for change. Among the various kinds of contact one of the most influential was warfare, the diffusion of ideas and especially techniques often taking place under the duress of military occupation. Following the Korean invasion of southern Japan in the third century AD, for example, Chinese jade-working methods were spread to the defeated islands by the conquerors,

95

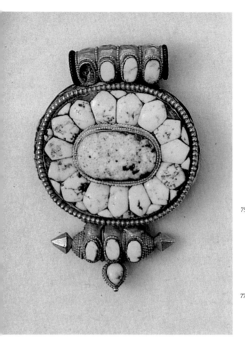

75 Gold amulet box from Tibet, encrusted with turquoises, and decorated on the sides with floral filigree designs. The container would have hung by chains or braids threaded through the tubular loop on the upper edge.

76 *Opposite* Manchu bridal head-dress from Qing China (19th century), adorned with kingfisher feathers glued to metal, and red coral and glass beads. At the crown can be seen the face of a mythological lion, silk flowers and a butterfly.

later to be followed by the knowledge of gilding bronze. Skills were also learned from subjugated peoples and many fine examples of Chinese metalwork date from the Tang dynasty (AD 618–907), when successes in Central Asia brought the empire into contact with cultures that already possessed a strong metalworking tradition.

World religions also had an impact on the design of jewellery. Different ethnic groups may, for instance, adopt similar aesthetic principles because of their adherence to the same belief system, as is especially the case with many societies that have come under the sway of Islam. The veneration of images is abhored by Muslims, and though their prohibitions on idolatry have never been invariably applied to secular objects, the paucity of figurative representations among many Islamic communities in insular South-East Asia can be traced back to religious strictures. Buddhist societies also share a common design heritage. Amulet boxes, for example, that contain religious relics or pieces of scripture are sometimes adopted as personal ornaments, while Buddhist sacred symbols and other religious motifs are often used to embellish jewellery.

Materials that are believed to have auspicious qualities are also widely used in the manufacture of personal ornaments, as is especially the case with jade. Associated with health and luck, and perceived as a link between heaven and earth, jade has long been the pre-eminent material of the Chinese people. Jade imagery permeates the language, a beautiful woman being known as a 'jade person' and 'fragrant jade' being a woman's skin. In imperial China the premier prize for athletes was jade, gold being reserved for the second place and ivory the third, while the tinkling of jade hanging from the belt was the sound of a gentleman.

Jade's significance remains undiminished, and in Xinjiang Province members of the Uygur ethnic group still hunt for nephrite boulders which are sold to the government for a fixed price. Not all this precious commodity finds its way to the capital, and some jade is carved in the provincial city of Hotan. Using treadles to turn a blade and applying sand as an abrasive, the artisans shape bangles, finger-rings, beads and other ornaments. Similar methods are used far to the south in Guangzhou (Canton) to make jade jewellery for export, much of which is sold via Hong Kong. The latter city is also a major destination, often illicitly, for another silicate that has similar properties to nephrite. Known as jadeite, or 'kingfisher' jade in Chinese (*fei-chi-yu*), this material began to be imported in significant quantities from Burma in the eighteenth century.

Like jade, ivory is one of the oldest decorative materials to be used in China, and bone, ivory's poor relation, also has an ancient usage. Hairpins of bone were used during the Shang dynasty (1600–1100 BC) and were still being made, often with elaborately carved knobs, in the early twentieth century.

Chinese metalworking also has a long history; bronze-casting, commonly with a lead alloy, was highly developed by the Shang period. Belt hooks cast in animal shapes were available during the time of the Warring States (475–221 BC) and an exquisite ornament of a crouching horse shows the use of silver around 300 BC. Interestingly, in China the technique of heating and then hammering metal (forging) is less ancient than casting, while the full potential of cold-working methods was not appreciated until the Tang dynasty (AD 618–907). An important innovation was the use of solder, an alloy of silver and copper, since it enabled complex ornaments to be assembled from many elements. Perhaps one of the most striking uses of metal was in jewellery worn by high-born women of the Qing dynasty (AD 1644–1911). Kingfisher feathers were glued to elaborate metal hair ornaments, from which were hung chains of pearls and semi-precious stones.

From the photographs and many written accounts that document the final years of Manchurian rule of the Qing dynasty, it is possible to ascertain how jewellery was worn by the gentry, the traditional Chinese upper class, and the members of the bureaucratic

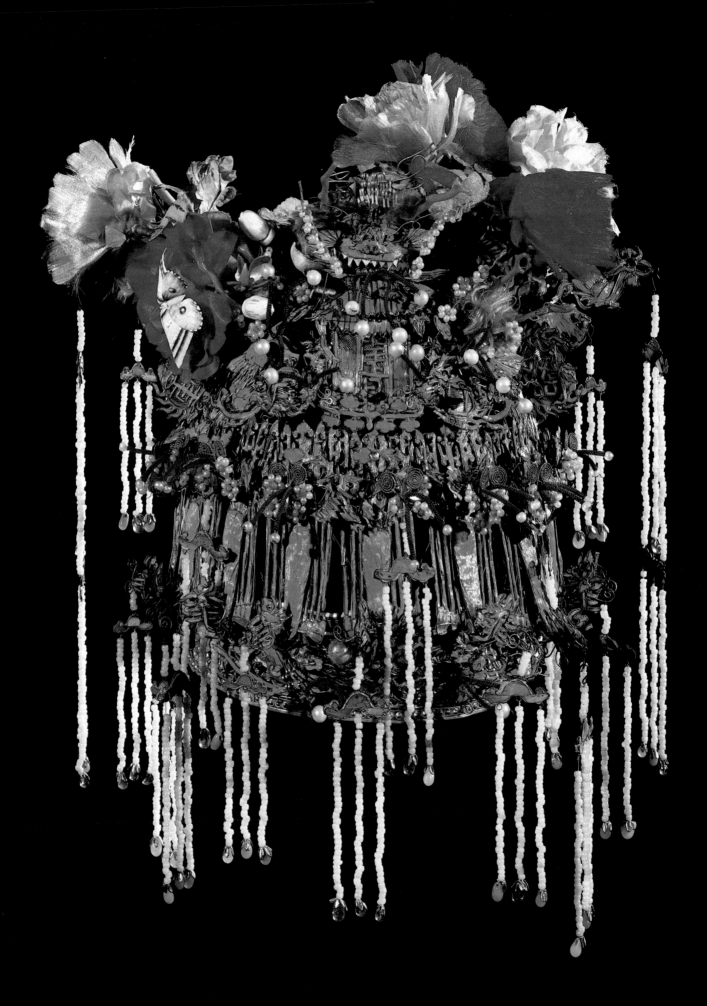

77 *Left* Jade pendant from Qing China (18th century). Made of carved jade plates linked together with cords, this pendant would have hung from the belt or sash of a member of the gentry, the traditional upper class.

élite. Bangles and finger-rings in jade, silver, opaque glass and ivory were used, as well as jade pendants and strings of fragrant seeds that were looped over robe fastenings. The elaborate hairstyles of the women were enhanced with combs, and ear-rings, often studded with pearls, were hung from pierced ears. While men's accessories were usually less complex than those of women, high-ranking civil servants wore long necklaces of coloured glass as part of the regalia of office. Plaques indicating that the wearer was foregoing certain food for devotional reasons were also worn.

Contemporary Chinese dress contrasts markedly with that of the last days of imperial domination. During the early years of Communist control little jewellery was worn, with the exception of official badges and medals, and under the Gang of Four concepts of personal adornment were severely criticised. Slowly, fashionable clothing has regained official approval and jewellery, albeit in limited quantities, can be seen on the streets of cities like Guangzhou (Canton). The jewellery styles of the Cantonese-speaking Chinese of Hong Kong are, however, markedly different. Mass-produced costume accessories such as sunglasses and digital watches are worn at all social levels, while the economic élite of this avowedly capitalist city sport personal ornaments bearing international design labels.

While jewellery is not, at present, an especially distinctive feature of ethnic Chinese dress, this is not the case with many of the republic's national minorities. Although the traditions of these peoples were often threatened during the Cultural Revolution, the policies of central government have become more sensitive in recent years. Jewellery is an essential feature of many of the costumes of the minority nationalities, especially in Yunnan in south-west China. Not only are the forms of dress worn in Yunnan symbols of ethnic affiliation, in what is China's most culturally diverse province, but the local costumes are the formal wear for these people. Regional outfits, complete with jewellery, may therefore be donned when visiting friends and relatives in nearby villages or for going to market in the local town (urban centres are usually multi-ethnic). National costumes are also worn in their full splendour during local festivals. Dai women, for example, of the Xishuangbanna region, wear jewellery on a regular basis, most noticeable being the silver belts worn over the sarong. On occasions such as the Dai New Year, additional ornaments are worn, including ear-rings and finger-rings, while plastic, silk or real flowers are placed in the hair.

Some of the most elaborate costumes of south-west China are worn by the Miao during their New Year festivities. Over dark clothing festooned with bands of intricate embroidery, the women wear numerous silver trinkets, while their hair is adorned with silk ribbons and flowers. Highly decorative costumes were also worn during the early twentieth century by Mongolian shamans. The highest class of these ritual specialists was thought to have supernatural powers and to be able to explain the will of heaven. During initiation ceremonies shamans wore numerous gleaming bronze plates and small bells which were attached to their clothing; streamers were also hung from the hat and the back of the coat. Although the Mongolians have a shamanistic heritage, their art forms reflect strong Buddhist influences.

In Tibet jewellery has long been a characteristic feature of costume, and this was especially the case with upper-class women until the mid-twentieth century. Sir Charles Bell, for example, reported that Tibetan '. . . ladies of good position' were known as 'gyen sang ma' or '. . . she with good ornaments', and period photographs show wealthy women in horned head-dresses, comprising a fabric stretched over a wooden or bamboo frame, from which decorations were hung. Ear-pendants, also an essential part of this costume, were not hung from the ear itself, but were hooked into the hair above.

Amulet boxes, sometimes with an opening to display an icon, were also worn by

78 *Below* Miao woman's neck-ring, typical of those from Burma, Thailand and Yunnan (south-west China). The ring is decorated with silver spirals and twisted wire. Silver jewellery is symbolic of the family's economic success.

79 Mongolian head-dress ornaments made of silver decorated with enamel and coloured stones. Mongolian peoples are today found in northern China, the Soviet Union, as well as the Mongolian Republic.

women, who hung them from necklaces or fixed them to their elaborate headgear. Images of Tara, who was believed to work swiftly against misfortune and disease, were popular, as well as Buddhist sacred symbols. Printed or hand-written charms, fragments of a monk's robe and other religious relics could be stored in these boxes.

Ornaments, some of which were equipped with leather ties, were also plaited into the hair, men sometimes wearing a long single braid to which jewellery could be attached. A woman's outfit could be enhanced with metal collars and the necklaces that reached well below the belt often supported a chatelaine. From these elaborate pieces, frequently embellished with cloisonné enamelling, were hung domestic implements such as tweezers and needlecases.

One of the distinctive features of Tibetan jewellery is the use of turquoise, a locally-obtained stone that is thought to have talismanic properties. Rings and bracelets were inlaid with this prized commodity, as well as special charm boxes that were worn by lay officials in independent Tibet. Furnished with cylindrical rings, these cases were used to hold a knot of hair near the top of the head. Set in either gold or silver, turquoises were given as wedding presents to brides who would wear them on a disc at the back of the hair.

In addition to turquoise, Tibetan artisans made use of a wide range of valuable materials including bright-blue lapis, jade beads and coloured glass. Amber necklaces were much esteemed, as were seed pearls and coral, the use of the latter having been remarked on by Marco Polo as early as the thirteenth century. Tibetan jewellers also

80 A gilt-bronze collar from Tibet (18th-19th century), set with inlays of turquoise, lapis lazuli and coral. Much Tibetan jewellery is characterised by a taste for 'exotic' imported materials, such as the coral of this piece, as well as pearls, amber and mother-of-pearl.

worked a wide variety of metals, ranging from inexpensive copper alloys, that were sometimes gilded, to silver and gold.

With the annexation of Tibet by China in 1950, the indigenous society was severely disrupted and during the Cultural Revolution many of its institutions and traditions were suppressed. Refugee communities living in neighbouring states such as India and Nepal have, however, kept alive many aspects of Tibetan culture, the skills of artisans having provided an important source of income. As well as the people of these host countries, visitors to the Himalayas have become keen buyers of the distinctive Tibetan jewellery.

Other forms of ethnic jewellery now sought by both foreign and local buyers are those worn by the diverse peoples of the region known as 'The Golden Triangle', the meeting point of Thailand, Burma and Laos. Fearing the inflationary tendencies of local currencies, the highland farmers of this famous region put their faith in silver, a precious metal that features prominently in much of the local jewellery. For these societies the family's wealth can be ascertained by the numerous silver ornaments that are worn, especially by women of marriageable age. This jewellery is also an essential part of the distinctive costumes that are worn partly for reasons of ethnic pride.

Although complex jewellery is used by the majority of these highland groups, perhaps some of the most striking is that of the Lisu, a people who straddle the borders of Thailand, Burma and Yunnan. The time when the most elaborate costumes are seen is during the New Year festivities, the start of which is announced by the local priest. Great effort is invested in ensuring that the young women are splendidly turned out. Black

101

81 *Left* Akha girl, a recent immigrant from Burma to Thailand, wearing an elaborate head-dress festooned with chased and repoussé silverwork, and numerous bead necklaces.

velvet vests, decorated with silver buttons, are worn with a cloth collar that supports numerous dangles, above which are placed layers of neck rings and necklaces. A silver chain, comprising several strands, passes under the chin from one dangle ear-ring to the other, while wide bracelets with bevelled edges are used to adorn the arms and numerous silver rings the fingers. In contrast, the men are more plainly attired, wearing only a silver ear-ring in the left ear, bracelets on each wrist and a jacket adorned with silver buttons.

Courtship in Lisu villages often takes place around the rice pounders in the evenings, bracelets being exchanged as love tokens. When going to a village to court a girl, however, a Lisu man will sometimes ask if anybody in the settlement is possessed by a weretiger (human being able to be turned at times into a tiger); association with even a relative of such a person is socially undesirable. It is also held that a possessed human can sometimes cause the essence of a weretiger to depart into a valuable object such as a silver ornament. The piece of jewellery may then be discarded on waste ground; but, anybody picking it up risks becoming possessed in turn.

In addition to silver many other materials are used by the peoples of the Golden Triangle. Brass and copper bangles are worn, as well as ornaments made from beads and shell. The Lahu, in particular, wear striking red and white beaded necklaces, while the Akha and Karen incorporate Chinese beads into their jewellery. Tourism is also having an impact on the design of jewellery, especially in northern Thailand where cheap varieties are made for sale to both Thais and foreign visitors. Some materials, such as aluminium, have found acceptance among some highland groups.

82 *Below* Karen jewellery from the Golden Triangle. A wide range of materials are used, here comprising a silver tiara and hairpin, brass and aluminium hairpins and bracelets, bracelets made of white buttons and boars' tusk combs.

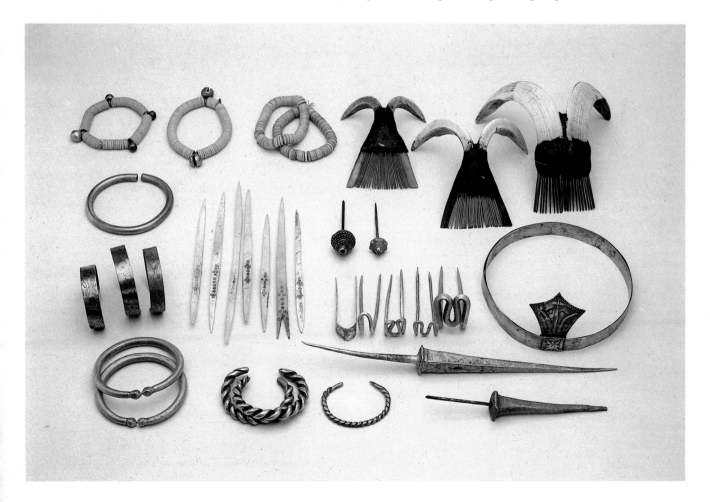

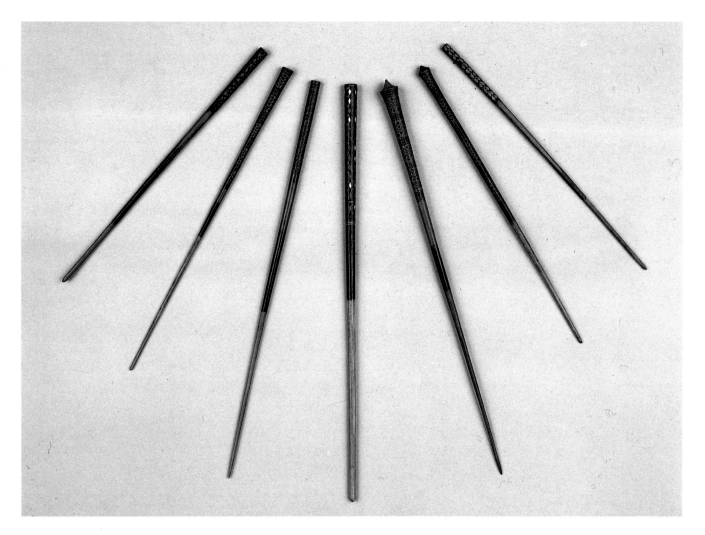

83 *Above* Wooden hairpins of the Haka Chin, north-west Burma (mid-20th century), decorated with geometric designs in red, grey and black. Such hairpins are worn in the back of the hair by Haka Chin women.

84 *Opposite* Iban children from north Borneo, dressed to celebrate the Rice Festival. Their finery comprises several necklaces and coin pendants, as well as leg-rings, armlets and bracelets worn by the boy, and anklets and a belt buckle embellished with chasing and repoussé on the girl.

By their appearance these highland dwellers can be distinguished from people, such as the Lao, who live alongside the Mekong River. Lao dancing girls may wear precious metal hairpins, ear-rings and finger-rings, and children are protected from evil by necklace amulets; but they do not adorn themselves with copious quantities of jewellery like, for example, the highland Akha.

Another border zone where ethnic minorities can be identified by their dress lies to the north-west of Burma. Among one of these people, the Haka Chin, jewellery is of great social significance and is included in the obligatory payments that precede a marriage. Old and beautiful beads, known as *pumtek*, have a high exchange value and confer prestige on the families that own them. Unmarried Haka Chin girls also wear *pumtek* in their coin-decorated necklaces, and coloured pins may be stuck in the back of the hair. Ornaments in brass and silver are also made in the Chin region by craftsmen who, though not professionals, work on a fairly regular basis.

Another South-East Asian region with a strong metalworking tradition is the Indonesian or Malay archipelago. Archaeologists have argued that these skills were acquired via contact with the South-East Asian peninsula. Although the excavations at Ban Chiang have demonstrated that the knowledge of bronze-casting is extremely ancient in Thailand, it is the styles and methods of a later culture, that of Dongson (*c.* 1000 BC) in Vietnam, that have more in common with those of the archipelago. In more recent history trade was undoubtedly important as a means by which ideas were exchanged and

affinities between the metalworking skills of mercantile cities, often predominantly Muslim, are apparent.

Although casting and cold-working techniques are used by the islanders to make jewellery, it is the latter methods that are the most widely used. Cold-working skills include the embellishment of beaten copper, silver and gold by chasing and repoussé, the fine details being later picked out with a punch and hammer. Designs may be engraved into these metals with sharp chisels and fine filigree work can be created with soft wire and solder. Granulation is also skilfully used to make complex patterns on the surface of ornaments.

The old courts of Indonesia made use of the skills of specialist artisans, as was especially the case in Yogyakarta and Surakarta in Java, and Klungkung and Gegel in Bali. Craftsmen settled close to the royal centres, members of the same profession usually residing in the same quarter. Workers in precious metals, the principal makers of high-status regalia, prospered under royal patronage and, in return for their services, were often awarded the use of royal lands, the yield of which they were entitled to.

Periodic displays of wealth and prestige were an essential feature of Indonesian courtly

85 Group of gold finger-rings from Java from the pre-Islamic period. They are variously decorated with cast or applied ornament in gold, engraving or semi-precious stones. The ring *top left* has a cabochon crystal, and the ring *bottom right* has a garnet, an amethyst and a crystal. The seal engraved on the ring *bottom left* shows a fish above a lotus.

life. Holy days in both Muslim Java and Hindu Bali were marked by parades, allowing the ordinary citizen a glimpse of regal authority. Dressed in their finest attire, the prince or sultan and his retinue would go to make their observances at the appropriate shrine, mosque or temple. Shielded by an umbrella, an important royal symbol, the monarch could be distinguished by his gold ornaments, headgear and gem-studded kris (wavy-bladed dagger). Music and dance also contributed to royal prestige, each capital usually having its own *gamelan* orchestra. The dancers themselves wore the finest costumes available, including gilded bracelets, anklets, head-dresses and beaten metal armbands.

Prized as a symbol of wealth, health and good fortune, gold is the foremost material of the Indonesian archipelago. Not only was this precious metal used, in the past, to make the jewellery of the ruling class, but it is still worn by bridal couples. Dressed in their finest regional costumes, the newly-weds receive the congratulations of relatives and friends at a reception held shortly after the marriage ceremony. Gold or gilded ornaments are included as part of the wedding attire among many ethnic groups, perhaps some of the most striking being those of the Makassarese and Buginese of southern Sulawesi.

The bride's long hair, worn piled on her head, is bedecked with gilded flower-shaped

86 Balinese girl dressed to perform the Butterfly Dance, photographed by Beryl de Zoete in the 1930s. Her head-dress has chased and repoussé decoration and the collar is filigree work; her arm ornaments represent wings.

and pearl-headed hairpins, while ear-rings are hung from pierced ears. Around her neck she wears a gold chain and from an elaborate necklace are hung medallions with repoussé patterns. Decorative metal plates sewn onto straps cover her upper arms, while her wrists and forearms are virtually concealed by numerous bracelets. Gilded hairpins are worn by the groom, while on his chest he may have elaborate medallions, including, perhaps, a gilded representation of a double-headed eagle, the symbol of the old Sultanate of Makassar.

As in other Far Eastern regions the Indonesians obtain many of the items they value through trade. Baroque pearls, much desired on account of their unusual proportions, and deep-red rubies are greatly in demand, and during the colonial period Dutch guilders were melted down for their silver. Not all Indonesian jewellery is, however, made from luxurious commodities. The thin branches of a black leathery sea coral, known as *akar bahar*, are, for example, twisted into decorative bracelets and, furthermore, are said to be effective against rheumatism.

Since the 1930s tourism, especially in Bali, has provided an important source of income for Indonesian artisans. Visits to workshops are regularly included in tourist itineraries in

87 Decorative comb, Maluku (Moluccas), eastern Indonesia. The comb has a mother-of-pearl inlay pegged to a wooden base, and was probably made in Kai.

Java, Bali, Sumatra and Sulawesi, and peddlars hawk bangles and rings around the resorts. Much of the jewellery made specifically for tourists is of mediocre quality; excellent work, however, is still produced for the local market and the more enterprising foreign buyers.

While beads are used as jewellery in many South-East Asian islands (China has long been an important exporter of glass beads) some of the finest examples of beads can be seen in the Philippines, particularly in the northern island of Luzon. Ceramic beads, either glazed or decorated with different hues of clay, are used, as well as glass beads coloured with metal oxides and minerals. Shell, seeds, bamboo, teeth and wood are also among the many materials included in beadwork. Beads may be threaded, especially on wire or horsehair, or sewn onto a piece of fabric or strong cord.

Bead necklaces are treasured as family heirlooms along with Chinese jars, plates and gongs, and among the Kalinga bead ornaments are sometimes deemed to have talismanic properties. The Ifagao also have necklaces, known as *anting-anting*, that are thought to impart good luck; these are made of teeth, while the Ubo use nautilus shells etched with designs as amulets. The root and tree-bark necklaces made by the T'boli are similarly credited with positive qualities and are believed to be efficacious in warding off sickness.

Bead ornaments are also used during the rituals that mark salient points in the life cycle. In the early twentieth century, for example, Igorot mothers would give their

88 Brass jewellery from Luzon, Philippines. The necklace has five cast elements bound together; the twined red and black cords can tie it round the neck. The ear-rings are made of coiled brass wire.

daughters head-dresses of agate beads, and when mature, the girl would receive a girdle decorated at the back with metal rings. Among the Kalinga a child is presented with a necklace, *balón*, to mark the occasion of its first visit to the house of the father's parents. Valuable beads were also given by go-betweens to the parents of a future bride, the first step in the marriage contract. A similar custom is followed by the T'boli, except it is the mother of the boy who places a necklace on the girl whom she hopes will one day be her daughter-in-law.

The noise-making properties of jewellery are also exploited by various Filipino groups. Some T'boli bracelets are, for instance, furnished with ball-bearings that make a sound as

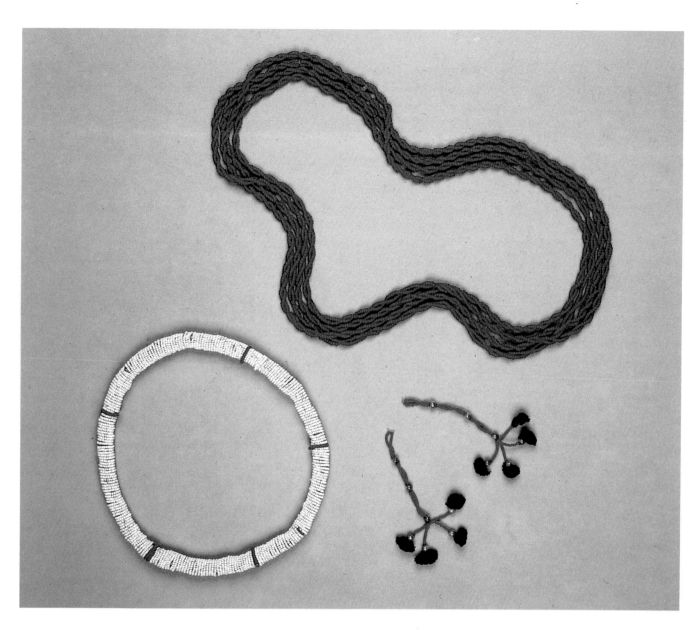

89 Bead ornaments from the Philippines: a pair of red bead pendants; a necklace of eight strands of tiny red beads twisted in pairs; a neck-ring consisting of a core of vegetable fibre covered with rings of white and red beads.

the wearer walks, and the bells that are hung from the distinctive brass or beaded belts signal the approach of a young woman eligible for marriage. Functional items are sometimes used as jewellery, such as the decorative bags worn by Kalinga men to hold their betel-chewing ingredients and other small objects. Further to the south on the Island of Mindanao, cosmetic containers, which are suspended from beadwork straps, are also worn.

Beadwork is included in the costumes worn by many ethnic groups in the Philippines. Wealthy Kalinga women, for instance, wear enormous necklaces of agate beads, along with ear ornaments of mother-of-pearl and brass. Their hair may be thickened by tying in switches taken from the tresses of dead female forebears or relatives with fine heads of hair. Bead chokers are worn by southern Kalinga men, while their northern counterparts have distinctive ear plugs, the front of which may be adorned with embroidered cloth, polished coins or pieces of looking glass. Flowers, such as the scarlet hibiscus and marigold, may be worn in the hair, as well as feather plumes. Brightly-coloured pieces of worsted are also worn as ear ornaments and early twentieth-century photographs show

90 A group of 19th-century Japanese lacquer *inrō*. The designs show (*top left*) a carp in black and gold lacquer, with transparent lacquer over gold leaf; (*top right*) a crayfish carved in cinnabar lacquer in high relief; (*bottom left*), also in cinnabar lacquer, plum blossoms and boughs in low relief, with matching ojime and *netsuke*; (*bottom right*) a parakeet in black lacquer with mother-of-pearl inlay. Two of the *inrō* bear the makers' marks.

the use of sugar cane leaves as ear-plugs by the Igorot. Some of the best examples of netted beadwork are worn by T'boli women as side pieces hanging from their hats.

In common with the Filipinos and other Far Eastern peoples, the Japanese include jewellery as part of the overall costume. Ornaments, which are often exquisitely executed, are not usually worn in copious quantities and are designed to harmonise with the kimono, the robe worn by both sexes. Some of the finest examples of these kinds of personal ornament were developed between the sixteenth century and the Meiji revolution (1868), a period during which a highly distinctive tradition emerged in Japan.

The decorative items of this era often had a practical value, one of the most character-istic ornaments having been the *inrō*. Originally devised as a container for the wearer's seal (a kimono has no pockets), the *inrō* was used to carry medicines and other personal possessions. Carved lacquer, a technique developed in China that probably came to Japan via the Korean peninsula, was favoured by the makers of these elegant costume accessories.

A carved toggle, *netsuke*, was used to suspend the *inrō* by a cord from the sash worn around the kimono and, though made by a different craftsman, was designed to correspond with the decorative container. The materials used by *netsuke*-carvers were, however, sometimes different and in addition to lacquer these craftsmen exploited the properties of native timbers such as Japanese cyprus, cherry, boxwood, *isu* (a dark-brown wood with a close grain), sandalwood and persimmon. Other materials included ivory, stag's horn and bamboo.

One of the most common forms of toggle carving was *katabori*, three-dimensional miniature sculptures, the subjects being drawn from legends and popular tales. Shoki the Demon Queller, equipped with a broad sword, was often depicted, as were the Seven Gods of Good Fortune. Humorous scenes were equally popular, including those of a fishergirl resisting the amorous advances of an octopus and a huntsman being flattened by a badger with a grossly enlarged scrotum. Another important form of *netsuke* was the rounded or 'rice cake' toggle known as *manju*. These were often inlaid or engraved, sometimes with the design pierced through to show a complex scene.

To cater first for the feudal lords and then later the emerging merchant class, specialist artisans settled in the growing cities. Distinctive styles developed in the different urban areas and it is usual to refer to various kinds of *netsuke* in terms of schools (Kyoto, Osaka and so on). The signatures of renowned artisans were also included on especially fine pieces, though these are not always an infallible guide to authorship. The fact that specialist craftsmen were sometimes permitted, in the late feudal period, to bear surnames like clan leaders, a right denied ordinary Japanese, provides an indication of the esteem in which the foremost artisans were held.

In addition to the renowned urban specialists, there were many ordinary artisans who produced decorative objects that had wide popular appeal. Originally disdained by the upper echelons of society, these items, known as *mingei*, became the subject of Japanese academic attention during the early twentieth century. Among the various ornamental forms were inexpensive varieties of the lacquer medicinal boxes, bracelets, rings and ear-rings made in precious metals, and ornamental hairpins known as *kanzashi*. Following the economic collapse that accompanied the débâcle of the Second World War and the subsequent intensification of industrialisation, many of these small-scale producers went out of business. There have, however, been various revivals, usually emphasising regional styles.

Combs and hairpins, used to highlight a woman's elaborate hairstyle, are another striking feature of Japanese jewellery. Some of these hair fashions were so complicated that, so as not to disarrange them, many society women slept on neck pillows. Although plain wood, especially boxwood, was the most widely used material in comb-making, some of the finest hair ornaments were painted or inlaid with mother-of-pearl. Tortoiseshell was esteemed, but expensive, deer and buffalo horn being cheaper alternatives, while red lacquer combs were highly fashionable during the Edo period.

As well as being fashionwear, combs have long been ritually significant in many regions of Japan. On her wedding, for example, a bride would bring with her a complex set of combs and, traditionally, a newly married woman inserted a comb in her hair, only throwing it away should she want a divorce. In Okinawa it was also the custom for a bride to go to the groom's house accompanied by her nurse, who placed a comb in the young woman's hair to show that she belonged to the new house. One ancient belief holds that the soul of the wearer lives between the teeth of the comb and today some Japanese are reluctant to pick up discarded or lost combs. Hair ornaments also have religious associations. In the past imperial princesses about to devote themselves to the god Ise would give up a comb to indicate their detachment from worldly values, and women continue to present old combs at Kyoto's Yasui shrine during the September Festival.

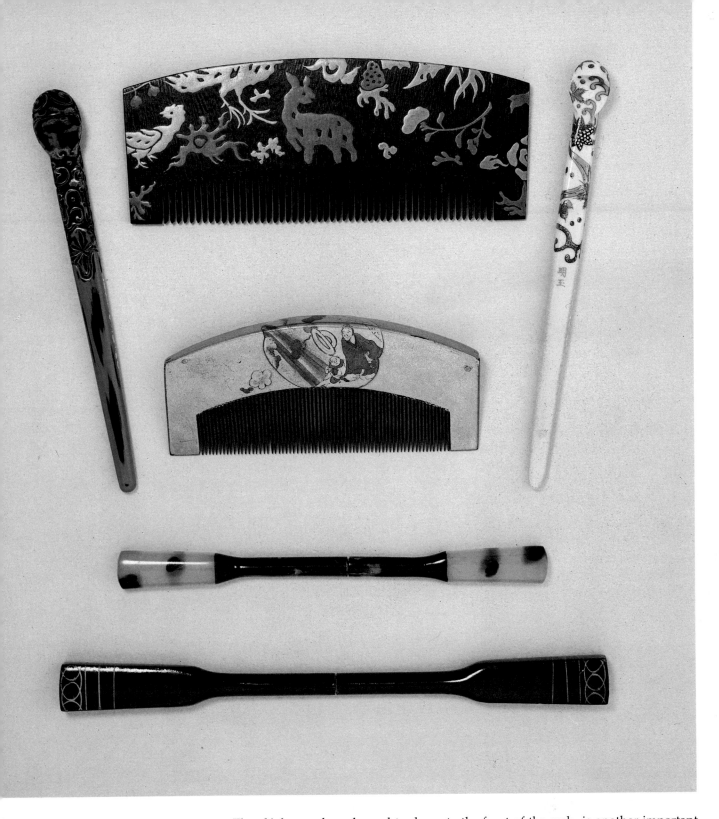

91 Women's hair ornaments from Japan. The two combs are of wood with gold lacquer; the pins are of red and black lacquered wood, ivory with gold lacquer, black lacquered wood, and tortoiseshell.

The *obi dome*, a brooch used to decorate the front of the sash, is another important ornament that is worn with the kimono. Other kinds of personal adornment, including brooches and rings set with precious stones, are worn to parties and other social events, but are not considered part of the costume that is worn on culturally significant occasions such as the tea ceremony. Today the Japanese, in common with many Far Eastern peoples, have access to an immense range of materials, often made by industrial processes, and techniques. Ethnic jewellery, however, continues to be a source of inspiration for designers competing in international markets, and remains an important indicator of ethnic affiliation and source of local pride.

4

The Pacific

♦

92 Comb from the Solomon Islands, made of lengths of tree fern and decorated with interwoven strips of orchid vine and coconut palm.

Jewellery is a term which in Euro-American cultures conjures up images of objects worn on the body and possessing high value, both as expensive commodities and as items worthy of being handed on from generation to generation. Within the traditional cultures of the Pacific basin similar kinds of objects existed. Some of the pieces described in this chapter, for instance, would be immediately recognised as 'jewellery' in exactly the same way that a diamond ring is. Others would be seen merely as worthless curiosities. This chapter surveys the range of items which could be described as 'jewellery' by those who wore them, with the emphasis, where the information exists, on the way they themselves regarded these items.

The Pacific region has never been culturally uniform. The region contains four main distinct cultural areas: Polynesia, Melanesia, Micronesia and Australia. These have been overlaid, in some cases obliterated, by intrusive colonial elements, mainly imposed by European powers; American and Japanese economic and political influence has also been increasingly felt in the period since the Second World War.

The relative emphasis in each of these areas on clothing, body decoration and 'jewellery' is different, as one might expect. In a broadly tropical environment body covering did not have a sheltering or protective function, but it was made to exploit its ornamental value; as such, it differed little from other forms of self-decoration. Tattooing was most highly developed in Polynesia, together, paradoxically enough, with various forms of enveloping clothing, most particularly in New Zealand. In Melanesia the use of personal ornament in close association with body decoration was common. In aboriginal Australia personal ornament took simpler forms, but body-painting assumed greater significance, particularly in the re-enacting of ritual dramas.

As has already been touched on in the introductory chapter, in examining the meaning of objects which are used to make statements about an individual's position in his or her social group, there is very little reason to separate 'jewellery' from other kinds of bodily ornamentation. All the objects illustrated in this chapter have been used to signify one person's social position in relation to others in their community, whether to dominate, entice or entertain. The great majority date from the period soon after European contact was first established.

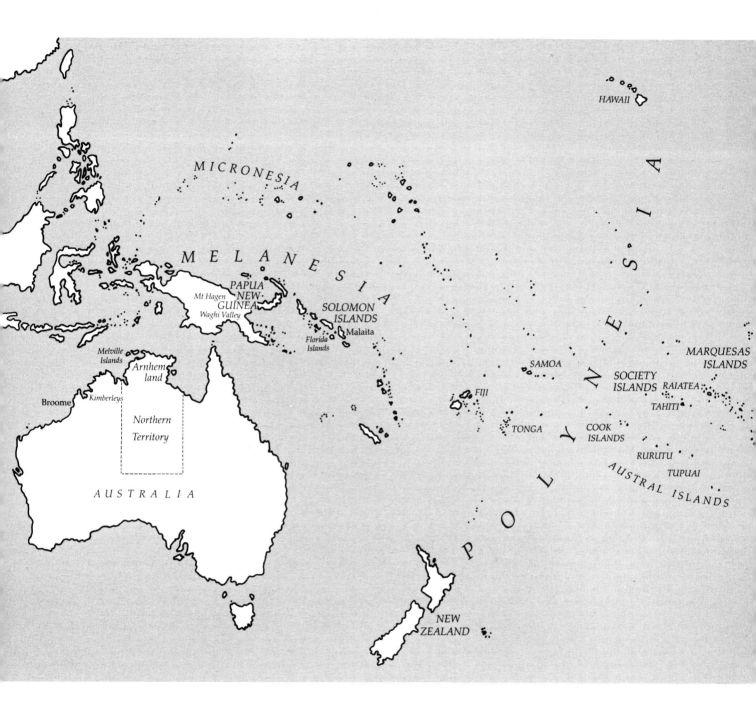

Map 3 The Pacific, showing the principal place-names mentioned in the text.

The significance of the jewel-like forms of body ornament in the Solomon Islands can be used as an initial example. As elsewhere, much of the emphasis in ornamentation is concentrated about the head – feather head-dresses, forehead and temple decorations, combs, nose ornaments and ear-rings. The other main category comprises waistbands, belts and armbands, the form of much of which had and has significance as money, or at least as a store of wealth. Head-dresses were worn exclusively by chiefs and consisted of the white feathers of the cockatoo and red feathers from a species of parrot. The most familiar and striking head ornament is known as *kap-kap*, made throughout the Solomon Islands and elsewhere in Melanesia. Although these objects are so well known, no detailed description exists of how they were made. Each consists of a disc of Tridacna shell (the giant clam), which provides a creamy white background to a striking circular design made from a thin sheet of turtleshell. There are usually several concentric bands of repeated radial designs, often using a four- to seven-pointed motif in the centre. Occasionally this incorporates human figures. Two especially fine examples obtained from Florida Island contain crouching images at the cardinal points, interspersed with other human-like forms. The detail and formal regularity in the design bespeak a high degree of confidence by the makers in their ability to control the material, which was most probably cut with abrasive wire. The discs were worn on the forehead, usually over the temple, attached to fibre headbands.

Combs were described as having been worn for effect, rather than merely being used to tease out the hair. A decorated comb with red streamers was one of the important items

93 Head ornament (or *kap-kap*) from Florida Island, Solomon Islands, consisting of a clamshell with a pierced turtleshell disc.

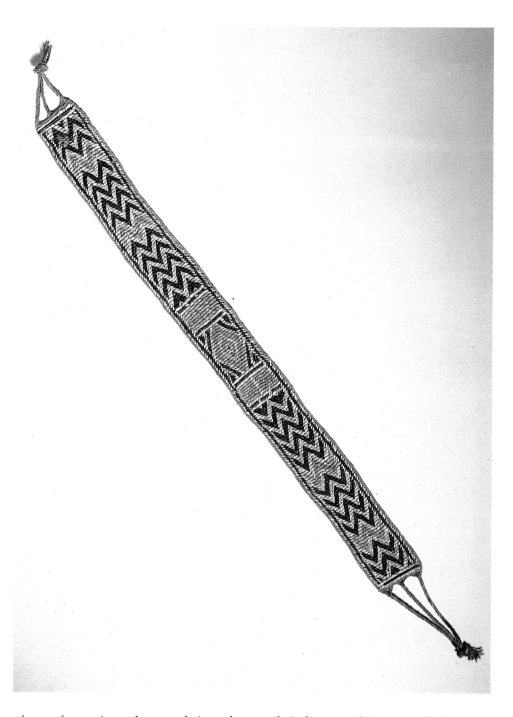

94 Belt of marine shell, with a turtleshell spacer at each end, from the south-eastern Solomon Islands.

of wear for novices who were being taken on their first expedition to catch bonito (a species of large tunny fish). Other obligatory ornaments were armbands and strings of red shell money. The combs were made up of finely shaped slivers of tree fern, decorated with plaited fibres of the yellow tissue of the orchid vine and coconut palm tissue dyed red. The armbands were also similarly decorated.

Belts occur in many collections. They are typically made of shell beads, the manufacture of which has frequently been described. Red beads come from the red Spondylus shell; black from the mussel, and white from species of Arca shell. These three colours have been used with great ingenuity to produce vibrant geometric designs, as well as frigate bird figures. Strands of such shells are strung together with the help of spacers of wood or turtleshell. Lengths of these bands constitute shell money. Human or animal teeth have also been incorporated into the belts. The use of these belts as money usually centres on the payment of bride-price, and for canoes, fees, fines and pigs. In Malaita the acquisition of lengths of shell currency was a preoccupation of many, since increased renown could be acquired through such transactions. However, this should not detract from their primary function as items of bodily ornamentation, since on special occasions the bands and belts could be worn ostentatiously.

One of the most extraordinary examples of ostentatious display is the profusion of headgear worn in the Mt Hagen area of New Guinea. Within the valleys enclosing a number of river systems a highly formalised gift exchange system was developed in which the major features were strikingly elaborate feather head-dresses. These are worn by men of the tribes of one area when they are involved in contact with other men in neighbouring areas. These men can spend the greater part of their lives organising such encounters in order to add to their own status within the community. The kind of events which require special costumes to be donned are warfare, courting parties, religious cults and exchange ceremonies. It is the last two in which the most elaborate decorations are worn and therefore where the greatest chance of status enhancement exists. Amongst the main items of exchange in the most important exchange ceremonies are polished discs of pearl-shell set into boards painted with red ochre, the rich matt shade of the ochre setting off the creamy lustre of the shell. They are worn on the chest on such occasions, but their main function is as valuables in their own right and a 'big man' gains status according to the number of such shell boards he can call into play during an exchange. Thus the boards are 'jewellery' in a very real sense, being thought beautiful, valuable and associated with high status. These exchange ceremonies, called *moka*, take years to organise. Formerly the organisation of the *moka* was so complicated and had to be done with such care that the planning meetings themselves were sufficiently significant for special costumes to be worn. For one of the dances in the exchange ceremony some of the men taking part wear a wig of plaited human hair into which is pinned a wicker superstructure serving as a base for several panels of feathers, from the lorikeet, waterfowl and white owl. The panels are separated by tall feathers of the King of Saxony bird. This structure is flanked by blue-bird feathers and surmounted by a crown of King of Saxony streamers. These plumes are especially rare. Indeed, they often in themselves form part of ceremonial gift exchanges. They were formerly only worn in the most
95 important gift exchange ceremonies between politically separate groups. The front of the wig is covered with a cut pearl-shell oval disc. The man also wears around his neck a tally stick of slats of wood, the length of which indicates the number of sets of pearl-shells he has given away. This is, therefore, an indication of his standing in the community. He often also wears a pearl-shell crescent around his neck. The whole outfit, completed by face-painting mostly in black with the eyes picked out in white and a long netted apron, is intended to be most arresting. This whole outfit is only worn by the men who are directly involved in the exchange of the mounted pearl-shell discs. The effect of a group of swaying dancers, the head-dresses effectively doubling the dancers' stature, each crown swaying majestically to the rhythm of the music, is hypnotic.

The main items used in body decoration are also considered to be valuable. They include pearl-shell, bailer shell, worn cut down or as enormous slices on the chest, the bases of Conus shell worn suspended from the nasal septum, cowrie shells worn strung as necklaces, Nassa shells sewn onto barkcloth bands and worn on the forehead. Other items, particularly feather plumes of the kind incorporated into head-dresses, also formerly had 'value'. Europeans altered this delicate structure of value by making these precious things more readily available, either through trading in them themselves, or by

95 Man from the Mount Hagen area, Papua New Guinea, wearing an elaborate head-dress of feathers, and a long tally of slats of wood hanging from his neck, indicating his frequent participation in exchange ceremonies.

opening up trade routes through which they could be more easily transported. In the past shells were traded into the Mt Hagen area from the southern highlands and the Wahgi valley, at the head of which Mt Hagen stands. Feather plumes were mainly the products of hunting, and were obtained principally by those families with access to and rights over good hunting grounds. These items became valuable as they passed along a trading route in the same way as diamonds accrue value as they are mined, shipped to international trading centres, shaped, set and offered for sale on the retail market.

Often, as a piece of jewellery is bought and sold, it increases in value. This did not happen in the Highlands, but did elsewhere in New Guinea. In the islands surrounding

the extreme south-eastern tip a system of formalised exchange existed which centred on
two kinds of items clearly to be included within the heading 'jewellery'. One, called
mwali, is an arm ornament made from the shell of a species of Conus from which the base
and the narrower portion have been removed. The shell ring is polished, and holes
drilled in it to accommodate strands of shell beads, seeds, and so on. The other item,
called *soulava*, is a long necklace of flat round beads made of red Spondylus shell,
containing a pendant made from a large section of a conical shell pierced around its edge,
from which hang threads of shells, and so on. In the network of ceremonial exchanges
called *kula*, the *mwali* were always and only exchanged for *soulava*, one type of item
rotating in one direction through trading partners ranged in a number of islands, the
other rotating in the opposite direction. This '*kula* ring' was in fact the centre of social and
economic life in the period up to the First World War, but its primary interest in the
context of this chapter is the way it demonstrates how this kind of 'jewellery' accrues
value and preciousness through exchange. The necklaces and armbands were sometimes
worn, the former by women, the latter by men in full dancing array. As the items became
more valuable, that is, as they passed from one exchange partner to another, the
likelihood of their being worn decreased; thus these objects are similar in another
important way to jewels usually kept in the bank vaults of Europe and America. The
necklaces and armbands were primarily to be possessed, and then only temporarily. It is

96 Shell jewellery from
south-eastern New Guinea. On the
left is a Conus shell armband
(*mwali*), and on the right a
necklace of shell beads and
sections (*soulava*). These were the
principal items in *kula* ceremonial
gift exchange.

97 *Left* Fijian chest ornament made of sections of sperm-whale ivory and pearl-shell.

such transient possession which delivered prestige into the hands of the temporary owner. As they travelled around the ring of exchange partners the objects themselves became more valuable, and acquired names and a history which each owner carefully remembered. The paradox is, therefore, that the short-term owner derived prestige from possession, but also from delivery to the next exchanger in the chain, provided that person had an object of equal value which to exchange.

There are also many examples of societies in the Pacific within which such manipulation of the value attached to objects could not be tolerated; these were mainly in Fiji and Polynesia, where traditionally the system of assigning status was not open to such tampering. In these communities ornaments served the function of 'badges' rather than valuables or antiques. The elegant neck and breast ornaments of high-ranking Fijian nobles can be taken as examples. They were made of polished sections of whale ivory or complete teeth. The teeth were usually arranged radially. Another ornament which was worn only by chiefs during important ceremonial occasions and in battle was a disc worn on the chest made up either of sections of whale ivory or pearl-shell, or a combination of both. Those made of whale ivory usually had three flattened sections pegged together into a disc, with a flattened top and a carved toothed edge. The pearl-shell examples are highly finished, the edge carefully smoothed and in some cases grooved. The most outstanding pieces are those which incorporate both materials, the gleaming lustrous pearl-shell in the centre surrounded by ivory pieces of deep creamy texture and hue lashed tightly with vegetable fibre. The quality of the workmanship seems to have paralleled the rank of the owner, but their precise function remains obscure. Another material which because of its rarity was worn only by high-ranking men was the golden cowrie, polished but otherwise unadorned. Cowrie forms were imitated in whale ivory. Whales were not hunted by Fijian fishermen before the period of European contact, but whale ivory became available in small quantities in the early years of the nineteenth century and its use was therefore confined to persons of status and influence. In the early post-contact years sperm-whale teeth were most sought after from the decks of the whaling ships. As the teeth became easier to obtain, breast ornaments and necklaces

98 *Below* Ear ornaments from the Marquesas Islands. The left-hand pair, carved from single pieces of whale ivory, were worn by men, while the right-hand pair, discs of shell with carved bone pins, were worn by women.

99 *Above* Head-dress from the Marquesas Islands, made of coconut fibre with elaborately carved turtleshell and plain tritonshell plates.

100 *Opposite* Necklace from Tupua'i or Rurutu in the Austral Islands, made of coconut fibre wrapped in finely plaited human hair, with nine carved pendants of bone, some of them human.

were made from them more frequently, but do not appear ever to have been common. Whale ivory was also highly prized in Samoa, ground into long curved pointed pendants.

Less is now known about the reasons behind the use of jewellery and ornament among the Polynesian communities than among their Melanesian counterparts. It would be fascinating, for instance, to have some idea of the purpose of Marquesan ear ornaments. How much more interesting it would be to add that extra dimension of understanding which knowledge of the wearer's regard for them would give us. As it is, we can only marvel at the quality of such workmanship.

The ear ornaments of various forms were worn by both sexes. They were made of whale ivory; those worn by men were made up of a disc with a separate asymmetrical needle-like extension, usually bearing a human figure in typically Marquesan pose. The head possesses a pair of large staring eyes, a nose with wide flattened nostrils, wide-open mouth, arms with large hands clutching the abdomen, short fat legs often bent at the knee. The version worn by women bore the same elements but in differing proportions, the disc being less prominent, the spike placed centrally, usually with two or three figures rather than one. Fine as these carvings are, some figures being less than a half an inch in height, they are less striking than the remarkable head-dresses known as *paekaha*, made up of curved plaques of turtle- and tritonshell on a plaited fibre band covered in

124

discs of the same materials. Each of the turtleshell plaques consists of one or more pieces lashed together, with human figures carved in repeated form all over the surface. It is possible that, like the heirlooms of other cultures, these ear ornaments and *paekaha* were regarded as family treasures rather than individually owned. Although these and other ornamental objects exhibited exceptional qualities of workmanship and taste, perhaps the most unusual object of this type is far cruder in execution, as well as being rarer. This is a wooden gorget covered in abrus seeds, seen and described by Cook as a 'kind of ruff'. Braids of human hair with pearl-shell discs attached may also have been made and used in the Marquesas, but they have been given a Society Islands or Austral Islands origin.

The use of human remains in ornaments has had a widespread distribution in Polynesia, not only hair for braid, but also bone. The connotations of the use of such highly charged raw materials can now only be guessed at, but doubtless the ornaments they are part of were regarded as influential sources of power. Unfortunately, their precise meaning has in many instances been lost. Among the most enigmatic pieces of jewellery to come from the central Polynesian islands is a small number of necklaces of bone elements, some human, carved into a number of emblems of power, for example a

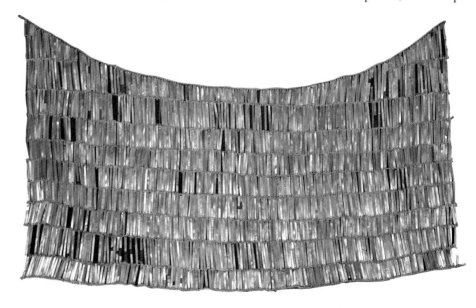

101 Breastplate from the Society Islands. Made of about 1200 thin sections of pearl-shell, it was worn as part of the costume of the chief mourner during funeral ceremonies of an important person (see 102 opposite).

pair of testicles, pigs (important in any transaction), chiefs' seats, all strung on human hair. They are thought to have been produced in the island of Rurutu in the Austral group, and to have been worn by high-ranking women or female chiefs. Concentration of impressive ornamentation reached its zenith in the islands of the Hawaiian and Tahitian groups. The death of a chief in Tahiti brought forth the appearance of an awe-inspiring apparition of the principal mourner, wearing a skirt of yards of barkcloth with a broad apron of small coconut shell plates. Above this was a breastplate of hundreds of minute slivers of pearl-shell, shimmering with every movement, suspended from a crescent of wood decorated with shell discs. The head of the figure was completely obscured by a mask of pearl-shell discs lashed together, showing no resemblance whatsoever to facial features, topped by an eerie spray of tropic bird feathers. Feather tassels hung down both sides like lifeless arms. This ghostly and fearsome creature also carried a pair of shell clappers to warn of its presence, which was supposed to bring death to any commoner unfortunate enough to set eyes on it.

The warrior/chief's costume from Tahiti, with its gigantic hat-like head-dress and

102 Complete mourning dress from the Society Islands, made of bark cloth and decorated with feathers, pearl-shell and coconut shell. The breastplate is shown in position.

103 U-shaped gorget is a further example of the ability of ornament to encapsulate the image of power. The overall impression created by these items decorated with precious materials such as sharks' teeth, feathers and dog hair on a wicker base was calculated both to increase stature and glorify the appearance of the warrior in combat, especially when seen from afar in a war canoe. The warrior's skill was less important than his ability in the performance of such roles. Captain Cook comments that the costume was 'designed more for shew than use'.

An outstanding example of a chief's head-dress is in the well-known print of the Rarotongan chief. He is wearing a head-dress of red feathers and human hair with a high feathered crest (an example in the Cambridge Museum of Archaeology and Anthropology is over a yard in height). The print shows not only the grace of the image but also gives details of the very fine tattooing patterns, including turtles depicted at the knees, and encapsulates the idea of the noble savage beloved of early nineteenth-century Europe. Another important element in this kind of image is a pair of rosettes, now thought to be from the Cook Islands, but originally described as warrior's shoulder

103 Breast gorget from Tahiti, Society Islands, comprising a basketry base with feathers, shark teeth and dog hair.

ornaments, from Raiatea in the Society Islands. They are made of twisted coir with tufts of the red feathers of the parakeet, similar to those in the head-dress.

A third example of an impressive head-dress restricted to use by the highest-ranking families is the *tuinga* from Samoa. It was made of bleached human hair on a barkcloth base, with an upright framework of wood slats decorated with feathers and a forehead band of nautilus shells. It was worn by chiefs themselves in time of war, otherwise only by nobles on festive occasions.

Feather girdles, referred to as *maru'ura*, worn only by the highest-ranking nobles in Tahiti, were the most extreme symbols of earthly and spiritual power, so much so that human sacrifices marked stages in their manufacture. The possession of a particular girdle was the reason for the outbreak of war on more than one occasion. Girdles were the embodiment of rank and political power, and are the most complete representations in ornament of the power of the chieftaincy to control life and bring death.

Of course not all forms of ornament in Polynesia served such significant symbolic

104 Nephrite neck pendants from New Zealand. The one on the left is carved as a human figure (*hei-tiki*), while the one on the right is in the shape of a fish-hook.

purposes. Illustrations of female dancers painted during Cook's voyages show delightful feather pompoms, and the wearing of flowers in the hair remarked upon then continues to be a feature today.

The use of 'found' objects as ornament was almost universal in Polynesia. In Samoa, most of the materials for ornamenting the body came from the flora of the islands and were worn on any occasion. In New Zealand high-ranking men stuck feathers in their hair, secured by simple carved wooden combs; if they could get them, the most sought-after feathers were the tail feathers of the *huia*, now extinct. Such was the rarity of these feathers that special boxes were carved and decorated to house them; these were passed on from generation to generation among high-class families. Perhaps the most unusual example of natural objects used as ornament was in New Zealand: the use of live birds as ear attachments, their beaks being thrust through holes in the lobe.

Of all the items worn on the body by the New Zealand Maori, the *hei-tiki* are the best known. More frequently worn by women than by men, they were made of nephrite

105 Neck ornament from the Hawaiian Islands; a pendant in the shape of a hook made of sperm-whale ivory on a set of loops of plaited hair.

carved in the form of a squatting figure, often female, but sometimes shown without sexual characteristics. The form of the figure on *tiki* is highly characteristic, head turned to one side, arms grasping thighs, eyes highlighted by pearl-shell inlay. The overall shape of the figure usually tapers from head to knees. At the time of the first European contact another form of neck pendant was also encountered; this was a piece of whale ivory cut with two eyes and strung on a cord from the root. Both forms were noted with about equal frequency, but by the middle of the nineteenth century the whale-tooth pendant had become much rarer than the *tiki*. This can be partially explained by reference to the origin of the greenstone for the *tiki*. In several unfinished examples in museum collections the origin of the material becomes obvious; the figures were carved from greenstone adzes, which had either become useless through age or had been technologically superseded by metal blades. However, the picture is complicated by the fact that the greenstone, being a precious material available in only one part of the country, was roughly cut into an adze shape before being transported, so this may have been the only shape available to Maori carvers. By the middle of the nineteenth century, the *tiki* had also become popular as an item of trade, since it was highly characteristic of Maori culture, made of a semi-precious stone, and easily portable.

A profusion of small and extremely delicate items of jewellery were carved by Maori craftsmen, not only from nephrite but whale bone, whale ivory, mudstone, steatite and wood. Bird-headed figures, seal, lizard, fish, oil and fish-hook forms worn as pendants were remarkable examples of carving on a small scale. Sharks' teeth were also worn, either actual examples or copies in nephrite. Although the *tiki* seem to have been worn more by women than men, the majority of other forms of personal ornament mentioned above were items of male adornment.

In the Hawaiian Islands the emphasis was not so much on the delicacy of carving lavished on small items, but on an overall resplendent effect, most spectacularly through the magnificent feather cape, topped by helmet-like head-dresses of feathers on a wicker frame. Generally the wearing of feathers was restricted to noblemen, but feathers were also incorporated into smaller female ornaments, like the *leis*, rings of feathers worn on the head or around the neck by high-class women. Leaves and flowers were also made up into such rings.

A great deal of care was expended in the manufacture of neck pendants in the form of a hook, usually suspended on a large number of finely plaited human-hair loops. The majority seen today were made of sperm-whale teeth or walrus ivory, but neither of these animals was hunted by Hawaiians before European contact; in any case walrus do not inhabit Hawaiian waters. The more common materials before European contact were either wood or, more rarely, human bone, and the earlier hooks were therefore smaller

106 Bracelets of boars' tusks from the Hawaiian Islands, worn by male *hula* dancers.

107 *Right* Armlet from the Hawaiian Islands made of turtleshell interspersed with plates of bone; the terminals are said to be of human bone.

108 Painting in the 'Mimi' style from the Cadell River area, Arnhemland, Northern Territory, Australia. It portrays a male figure with weapons, and wearing a large head-dress.

than the later ivory examples. In all cases the form was extremely graceful and the finish very smooth. The pendants were worn exclusively by women.

Other kinds of small ornaments were also made of whale and walrus ivory, such as small toggles in the shape of turtles, birds, hemispheres or shells. Bracelets of sections of 106 boars' tusks occasionally interspersed with turtleshell plates were rendered beautifully smooth and even in appearance by continued wear. Although in some early examples the tusks were not cut down, the majority were made up of tusks carefully graded in size and thickness. They were crown-like in form. Even more finely wrought were bracelets 107 made of fine plates of turtleshell, some of which were not much thicker than a coin, with plates of bone inserted at intervals; one or two examples of these bracelets have protruding terminals carved into human heads. Generally speaking, however, Hawaiian ornament is characterised by an unadorned and highly polished finish.

The male dancers of *hula*, as well as wearing the boars' tusk bracelets, wore leg ornaments of bands of fibre with rows of dog canines. In some specimens as many as a thousand teeth have been used; this points to the former widespread occurrence of the Hawaiian dog, now extinct (it was principally bred for food).

The kinds of ornament formerly used by the aboriginal inhabitants of Australia show much greater emphasis on the use of pigments and feathers added direct to the body in order to decorate it. There is, however, a rich record of paintings which show the former use of ornaments, mostly from the Northern Territory. Many of the earliest figures from 108 Arnhemland, in the 'Mimi' style, show elaborate head-dresses protruding in a long arc from the body, as well as armlets, waist ornaments and dancing skirts, worn almost exclusively by men. These are also depicted on some of the so-called 'Bradshaw' figures in the Kimberley area of Western Australia. Within the last forty years men and women of Melville Island have worn rows of bangles woven from human hair on a cane base, some decorated with abrus seeds, some with feathers. These are worn today as a sign of mourning, particularly for an important or well-liked person. Decorated pearl-shell 109 plates are reserved for wear on ceremonial occasions, either to pacify disturbed spirits, or to accompany important gift exchanges. There are other examples of use, but usually they serve to signify the importance of the ceremony and of the wearer's part in it.

The forms and contexts of personal ornaments changed drastically in the decades after the European presence began to be influential, largely through the baleful effect of zealous religious converts. Any kind of addition to the strictly functional use of clothing as bodily covering bespoke levity and was therefore to be discouraged. In recent times the pervading viewpoint has become more relaxed, but this has merely meant that tourists to most parts of Polynesia expect to be welcomed with garlands of flowers. The rich profusion of past times has been almost totally lost, at least in action; many fine pieces can still be seen in museum collections, but not on the very place they were made for – the body. This is not to denigrate the role of museums in preserving such valuables, and not to wish for a return to the olden times; apart from being undesirable, it would clearly be an impossibility, since many of the materials used so ingeniously – human hair, sperm-whale teeth, and so on – are not available. What is a cause for regret is that the same kind of ingenuity is not today being directed by the indigenous peoples of the Pacific towards the imaginative use of readily available materials in unexpected ways, as their ancestors so skilfully did.

109 Pearl-shell pendant with incised and blackened designs suspended from a waist-belt of plaited human hair; worn only by initiated men of the Pidunga people, Broome peninsula, Western Australia.

5

The Americas

♦

PRECOLUMBIAN AMERICA

110 Central American bird pendants of cast gold are the best known of extant Precolumbian jewels. Considered to represent birds of prey, the pendants first appeared on the Isthmus at about AD 500 and continued to be made until after the discovery of America. Christopher Columbus first reported the pendants in 1502.

In the three thousand years that preceded the European discovery of the New World civilisations of social complexity and intellectual accomplishment flourished on both American continents. The civilisations of Mesoamerica and Peru were the most successful of them, but countless other American groups were significant in the larger panorama of the Precolumbian New World. Personal adornment was an extremely important aspect of individual status for all ancient American peoples, and although their cultures differed widely in many respects, there were basic similarities in many of the forms of their ornaments and the materials of which they were made.

Mesoamerica in Precolumbian times stretched from northern Mexico to northern Honduras, and included two important cultural areas, the Mexican area to the north-west of the Isthmus of Tehuantepec and the Maya area to the south-east. Although their cultures were distinct and individual, the Mexican and Maya peoples may have had a common intellectual 'ancestor' in the Olmec of the Mexican Gulf Coast, and they were closely allied in many aspects of life and thought. In both areas personal adornment reached extraordinary heights of inventive elaboration. All manner of materials were used in decorative schemes that ranged from the austere to the grandiose.

The people credited with making the first important jewellery in ancient America are the Olmec, a group that lived at the turn of the first millennium BC along the lowlands of the Gulf Coast and who spread their influence widely throughout Mexico. The Olmec worked in jade, producing many personal ornaments – beads, ear-flares, pendants, masks – of the hard, polishable stone. American jade is jadeite, a pyroxene, and while known in a range of colours from almost white to almost black, shades of green were principally worked in ancient Mexico. The significance of the colour cannot be underestimated, for in Precolumbian Mesoamerica green was equated with water and vegetation, and greenstones themselves came to be the very symbol of preciousness. Greenstones, whether jadeite or other jade-like stones, were valuable throughout Mesoamerica's long history from Olmec times up to the Spanish Conquest.

Although it is jade for which Mesoamerican jewellery is most renowned, many other materials were used during the Precolumbian centuries. Obsidian, quartz, pyrite,

GREENLAND

ALASKA

CANADA

Rockies

Vancouver
Island

Great Lakes

UNITED STATES
OF
AMERICA

Pueblo Bonito

Mississippi

Apalachian Mts

Bahamas

Yaxchilan

HONDURAS

MEXICO

GUATEMALA

COSTA RICA

PANAMA

COLOMBIA

ECUADOR

Amazon

PERU

BRAZIL

BOLIVIA

PARAGUAY

CHILE

ARGENTINA

Map 4 The Americas, showing the
principal place-names mentioned
in the text. The numbered key
refers to the North American
Indian cultural areas.

1   Arctic
2   Subarctic
3   North-west Coast
4   Plateau
5   Plains
6   North-eastern Woodlands
7   South-eastern Woodlands
8   California
9   Great Basin
10 South-west

111 The distinctive facial features of the Olmec peoples of the Mexican Gulf Coast are evident in this mask of blue-green jade, the colour preferred by the Olmec for their jade objects. Made during the first half of the 1st millennium BC, the mask was probably worn as a chest ornament. Its side flanges were broken off in ancient times.

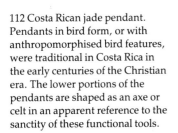

112 Costa Rican jade pendant. Pendants in bird form, or with anthropomorphised bird features, were traditional in Costa Rica in the early centuries of the Christian era. The lower portions of the pendants are shaped as an axe or celt in an apparent reference to the sanctity of these functional tools.

turquoise, shell, bone, gold, silver and pearls were among the more permanent, but ephemeral materials like wood, basketry, feathers, seeds and even paper were incorporated into personal decoration. None, however, not even gold, ever surplanted jade as the most valued of substances. When the Spaniards arrived in Mexico in the sixteenth century the wearing of jade was restricted to the nobility. Jewellery from Mexico which was sent back to Europe was greatly admired, and its exotic novelty appears to have influenced continental jewellery design for some decades.

Jade was also worked in the lower Central American region of Costa Rica from about 300 BC. The chiefdoms of Central America never grew as powerful and centralised as the city-states of Mesoamerica; wealth was amassed on a more modest scale, and this is reflected in the personal ornaments. In Precolumbian times the isthmus joining the two continents was the meeting-place of cultural influences from Mesoamerica and South America. The different traditions can be seen from variations in their artistic imagery and their preferences in materials. Goldworking, for instance, originated in South America, and was introduced into Central America, apparently by sea, in the early centuries of the first millennium AD.

At the time when gold jewellery became fashionable in Central America jade was dying out. Gold was then to be a valued personal possession and an indicator of rank and status until America was discovered by Columbus. In 1502, on his fourth voyage to the New World, Christopher Columbus saw gold pendants being worn by peoples along the coast of Costa Rica and Panama, including the so-called eagle pendants. While it is possible that gold and gold ornaments were considered to be protective of their Isthmian owners and wearers, the eagle pendants, which depict birds of prey, may further have been viewed as guardian emblems. Bird imagery also appears in the gold jewellery of adjacent Colombia, although details differ.

In the Andean countries of Colombia, Ecuador and Peru in north-west South America

important Precolumbian cultures flourished, but in Peru the concentration of political power led to the formation of kingdoms where great wealth was amassed by the few. Peru is also the source of the earliest evidence found so far of metalworking in South America: thin sheets of plain gold foil, dating to about 1500 BC. By the first millennium BC impressively large golden ornaments were being made. The crowns, pendants, ear ornaments and beads being produced were types which would for the most part continue in vogue for the next two thousand years, although details of their shapes changed over the centuries. Silver was also used, although many fewer examples of silver jewellery remain today. A number of ornaments combine gold and silver in one piece, indicating an interest in the colour effects of the different metals. Copper, when made into ornamental forms – it was extensively used for utilitarian items and tools – was usually surfaced with a layer of gold or silver. Sophisticated surfacing techniques were employed in Peru early in the first millennium AD. The alloying of metals, particularly gold and copper in a mixture known today as *tumbaga*, was practised in many of the American metalworking areas.

Organic materials have survived in the extraordinarily arid environment of the Peruvian coast in greater quantity than anywhere else in Precolumbian America. The objects of wood, fibre, feather, textile and hide which have survived thus offer insight into the multitude of adornments made and worn in ancient America that do not remain today. Colourful tropical bird feathers, impressive animal teeth and claws, delicate bird and fish bones, iridescent beetle wings, lustrous human hair, multi-hued plant fibres, sea shells – natural and worked – seeds, nut shells and fur are among the many materials that were used, but they seldom endure. Mosaic-work of feathers, shell or stone that

113 *Above* One of the earliest gold crowns (*c.* 500 BC) known from Precolumbian America, this tall, slender, Peruvian head ornament is embossed with the image of the so-called Staff God. The frontal, staff-bearing figure has a feline face on its torso and its own fanged mouth indicates deification.

114 *Right* An ornament from Peru, made from the smoothed half of a spiny oyster (Spondylus) shell during the first half of the 1st millennium AD. A figure is worked in a mosaic of bone, shell and stone, adding another dimension of colour to the piece. Remnants of the original suspension cord are visible at shell's edge.

115 Beads of orange-pink Spondylus shell form the background of this impressively large collar, some 17 inches high. Probably part of a matched set of ornaments that would have included cuffs, the collar was made in northern Peru in the 15th century. The stylised figures with raised arms are made of white and purple shell and green malachite beads.

114 decorates a range of objects made from a variety of materials do remain today. Mosaic
120 adorns wood ear-flares, or sets of ornaments containing larger items like collars, cuffs and crowns. Similar groups of objects were also decorated with shell beads, often made of the orange-pink Spondylus shell. The Spondylus, or spiny oyster, came from Ecua-
115 dorian waters and was imported into Peru, where it was much prized for both economic and religious reasons from at least as early as the second millennium BC.

Throughout the Precolumbian period personal ornaments made by American peoples had many features in common, although materials and specific details of shape and construction may have varied. Some areas of the body were decorated with regularity. The head and chest were understandably the primary focus for attention, and ornaments were made for the forehead and the top of the head, the ears, nose and lips, and the neck and chest. Labrets, or lip-plugs, were the least favoured of facial ornaments, although they were made intermittently on both continents. Waist, knees and ankles received a certain amount of decorative attention, particularly in Mesoamerica, but American arms and hands as a rule were scantily embellished. Bracelets and cuffs were few overall, but finger-rings were rarer still. Archaeological evidence suggests that they were reserved for the most politically powerful men. Feet could be encased in fancy sandals, but they do not actually seem to have been bejewelled.

The commonest personal ornament, as might be anticipated, was the necklace. It could consist of a single thong or cord on which an ornamental or magical object was strung, or it could be a multi-strand extravaganza so large that it covered the chest. The earliest archaeologically documented American ornaments are stone disc beads, perforated for suspension. On both continents such beads date to at least the third millennium BC, and similar beads of shell were probably made at the same time, although none survive. Another basic form of bead was the smoothed and perforated pebble, apparently ancestral to the round or spherical bead that was made in countless variations over the centuries. Tubular beads, both long and short, were numerous, and even square and

116 Beads excavated in a 9th-century BC burial at Copan, Honduras, have been restrung in a semblance of their original order. Four such 'necklaces' had been placed in the same burial. The claw elements refer to the jaguar, power symbol *par excellence* among early Mesoamerican societies.

117 Metalworking began only late in Precolumbian Mexico, but by Aztec times (14th–16th centuries AD), the Mexicans were expert goldsmiths. This intricately detailed ornament, cast by the lost-wax process, may have been but one element of a larger multi-part pendant. Such elaborate works of gold greatly impressed the conquering Spaniards when they arrived in the New World.

118 The Tairona peoples of Colombia produced virtuoso castings primarily of a gold-copper alloy known today as *tumbaga*. This *tumbaga* pendant figure, with his great jutting jaw and enormous head-dress, wears many facial embellishments. Two types of ear ornaments are worn in his ears, a lip-plug adorns his impressive chin and a nose ornament dangles from his nose.

rectangular shapes were produced in stone. Pearls and precious metals were also used for beads. Pearls survive burial poorly, however, while silver beads hardly survive at all. Gold beads, on the other hand, remain in some quantity, particularly in Peru, where they were a much favoured ornament in ancient times. Commonly made of hammered sheet gold, Peruvian beads were fused or soldered together when constructed of numerous parts. These beads reached very large sizes – some are almost as large as tennis balls – by the late preconquest centuries. Whether or not the large beads were meant to be worn in life or had a purely funerary function is not known.

Information is scant on the nature of the finished stringing of the beads and other necklace elements. Except in those areas where contemporary depictions illustrate them, such as the Maya reliefs, or where stringing arrangements have survived burial, as in 116 regions of Peru, Precolumbian necklace design is problematic. In modern times many ancient necklace components have been restrung in totally haphazard manners that obscure their ancient character. Intact Precolumbian necklaces, when remaining condition allows, illustrate greater craft, conceptual inventiveness and finish of presentation than are found in the modern reconstructions.

The simplest pendants – perforated objects of minimal outline – were made long before pottery was produced. Many of these are presumed to have been magical or protective in either material or function, or both. Subsequently this minimal ornament was extensively elaborated and by late preconquest times technically and visually complex objects were being produced. Seldom more than eight inches high, most surviving Precolumbian pendants are of stone or gold. Carved shell and bone examples, sometimes with incised designs, remain in smaller quantities; countless other pendants of perishable materials were produced. Archaeological evidence suggests that the ornaments were individually hung or strung in informal groupings with beads and other small items which may have had symbolic as well as decorative significance.

In Mesoamerica the preferred material was jade or other jade-like stones, whereas in Peru it was gold. The pendant did not enjoy great favour in Peru, however, although it did so in all the other areas considered here. In Colombia and Central America, for

119 Cast-gold pendants that incorporate elements of other valued materials, such as precious or semi-precious stones; were popular in Panama in the mid-1st millennium AD. This dynamic pair of 'crested crocodiles' have inset tails of pink quartz. When worn, the least expressive aspect of the crocodiles, their backs, was visible. The pendant was hung from rings under the front feet.

instance, pendants became very elaborate, with great stylistic and formal diversity. Although human and animal figures were the basis for the imagery, the designs may show distinctly abstract qualities and a certain amount of fantasy, presumably based on mythological concepts. Among the Central American pendants are precious metal objects that have non-metal parts. Quartz, shell, pyrite and even emeralds were incorporated into gold objects, and the combination of different colours, textures and surface finishes add an extra dimension of subtlety to the pendants. Such felicitous pairings of precious metals with other materials happened relatively infrequently in Precolumbian America, but such work, described at the time of the Spanish Conquest, was produced in Aztec Mexico. The greenstone pendants of Mesoamerica frequently took the form of small masks. These were worn individually, as the central elements of collars, or as belt-masks. Belt decoration was a feature of important male costume. Collars, wide shoulder-to-shoulder ornaments connecting at the back of the neck, were made from numerous materials. Many are made up from beads, while others were in precious metals – large sheets of gold, dazzling in their impressive size. Important central elements were added to the collars as personal insignia. Small masks, without eye- or air-holes and thus not wearable, were frequently among these central collar elements.

Deity images and what may be ancestral portraits were represented. Pectorals, chest-sized ornaments suspended under the chin, were meant to be as conspicuous as the collars. Those made in the first millennium AD in Colombia were particularly grand, and they were part of the matched sets of gold ornaments that included head-dress frontals and arm decorations. Pronouncedly and intentionally ostentatious, these were ornaments fit for royalty and the semi-divine.

Head-dress ornaments were made to be attached to headbands, turbans or other basketry-type supports. They were imposing objects and usually included some kind of face – deity, human, animal, bird – as the main element, which was attached centrally over the forehead. These faces ranged widely in type and material. There are those that included actual animal parts, like the muzzle and bared teeth of a fox. When the muzzle was attached to a turban with a tail at the opposite side the whole head-dress 'became' a fox. Although organic parts seldom survive, it is probable that countless head-dresses of this kind were made in ancient times. Fox or feline faces in gilt copper or gold may well have replaced actual ones on the headgear of a person of sufficient rank and importance. The head-dress ornaments that endured in Mesoamerica are those made of jade and other jade-like stones. An unusual form of ornament used by the Maya consisted of thin

120 The brilliantly hued feathers of tropical birds were much prized in Precolumbian America for luxury items of all sorts. The feathered ear-flares of Peru are among the more personally scaled of such items; those here have carefully made feather mosaics on their frontals. The flares were made in the last centuries before the Conquest and the feathers were attached by means of an adhesive and cut to shape.

plaques of jade carved on both sides and attached perpendicularly to project straight out from the head-dress.

The wearing of ear ornaments was very common in Precolumbian times. Primarily disc-shaped ear-flares mounted on a supporting shaft, they were worn through distended ear-lobes. Mesoamerican examples were made from jade or jade-like stones, but some were of obsidian. This naturally occurring volcanic glass was extensively employed in Mesoamerica for utilitarian purposes, and it was put to ornamental use only sparingly until late in preconquest times. Peruvian ear-flares are quite similar in shape to those of Mesoamerica, although they were rarely made of stone. Numerous Peruvian ear ornaments are made from more fragile materials, such as feather and shell mosaics on wood

120

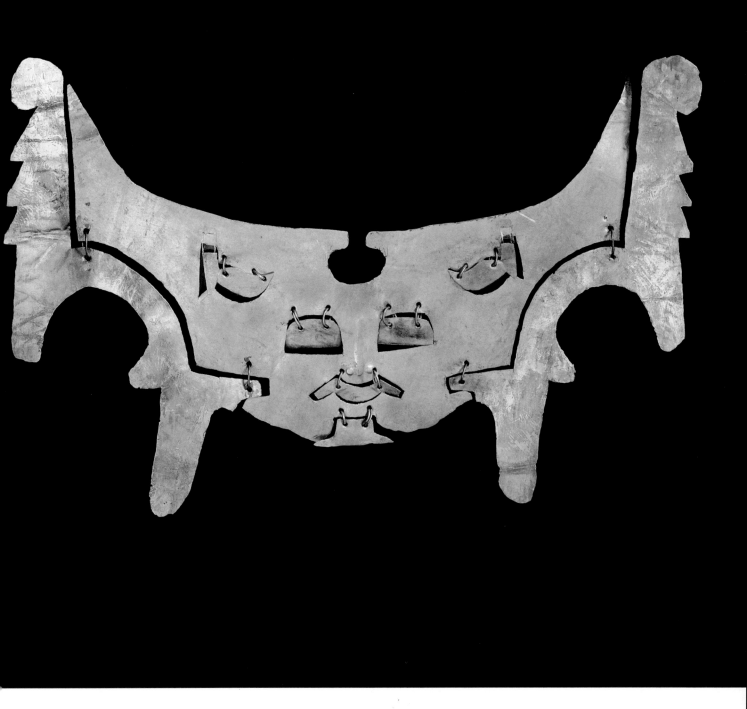

121 Gold nose ornaments of all sizes and shapes were made and worn in northern South America in ancient times. This sheet-gold ornament, made in Colombia in the 1st millennium AD, was worn suspended from the septum and covered most of the lower face of the wearer. The added parts, attached by means of tiny rings, further moved and vibrated when worn.

or bone. Others had gold elements in the mosaic designs to add to the variety of colour and texture. The most flamboyant Peruvian products were ear ornaments made totally of gold. These jewels reached great sizes: some frontals were as wide as five inches across, with multi-figure scenes attached to them; long counterbalancing shafts hung down behind and were covered with incised designs.

Nose ornaments – or nose-rings, nose-beads, and mouth-masks as they are also called – were another American favourite. Those of gold, chiefly South American, make up the largest number. Mesoamerican examples of jade were made, but they are few compared to those of precious metal. The earliest examples are delicate lightweight Peruvian objects that clipped onto the septum, thereby dangling from the nose. These were

routinely made from hammered sheet gold, a technique preferred in Peru throughout its preconquest history. In Colombia nose ornaments were both hammered and cast, and lost-wax casting was used there as elsewhere in Precolumbian America. Some Col-ombian nose ornaments are of such shape that they appear unwearable to a modern eye, although depictions on ceramics show these ornaments being worn in a very distended nose. Sheet metal ornaments that dangle from the nose and consequently swing or move when worn make an artistically interesting group. The potential for movement clearly intrigued their makers, and it became a focus of further elaboration.

Crowns, caps and diadems exist in gold and silver, and while the shapes may have been reproduced in other materials such works no longer survive; the supports are gone and the sheathing materials remain only as pieces. Plaques of jade are known to have decorated crowns, and it is possible that shell and bone plaques did the same. Simple headbands with some kind of central ornament, and special headgear, like the extra-ordinary feathered head-dresses of Peru, were undoubtedly more common than their scant remains suggest today.

The best illustrations of the manner in which ancient Americans adorned themselves can be found in contemporary images of Precolumbian peoples. Maya relief sculptures and vase-paintings of the first millennium AD, for example, convey a great deal of information about the personal ornaments of both men and women. Maya personages wore a great variety of costume, at times ceremonial and at times personal, and the ceremonial regalia was as imposing as any ever created in Precolumbian America. Much of the relief sculpture done in the eighth century in the Maya city of Yaxchilan on the Usumacinta River in Mexico depicts ceremonies in which the rulers of the city partici-pated. The Maya nobility is arrayed in full panoply, well illustrating the personal decorative impulse at its symbolic height. One such sculpture, dated to AD 709, shows Lady Xoc, principal wife of Shield Jaguar, a ruler of Yaxchilan. She is dressed with great care in a costume appropriate to the solemn significance of a sacrificial ceremony. While many elements of her regalia were prescribed by the specific ceremony in which she was participating, the refined delicacy of her jewels as depicted in the Yaxchilan relief transcends the prescriptions of ritual: they are elegant works of art.

Few Precolumbian peoples embellished themselves with quite the panache of the eighth-century Maya. Indeed, others espoused understatement in their personal adorn-ment, but most ancient Americans fell between the two tendencies in their efforts at self-aggrandisement through personal embellishment. Some types of ornament and materials, as we have seen, were appropriate to certain groups in society. For example, at the time of the Spanish Conquest jade in Mesoamerica and gold in Peru were reserved for the nobility, and prohibitions of all sorts undoubtedly existed on a multitude of other materials, restrictions that must have changed over the centuries. Distance and rarity, added to the value of materials in Precolumbian times as they do today. Shell, for instance, was traded far from its watery place of origin. Feathers also, particularly the brilliantly coloured raiment of tropical birds, must have been a luxury item from their earliest use: of necessity these, too, had to be traded into highland and coastal regions. Certainly twentieth-century feather ornaments made by the Tropical Forest peoples of South America, and still worn today, abundantly illustrate the glamour and potential inherent in these vivid, weightless treasures.

122 *Above* The jewellery worn in the early 8th century by Lady Xoc, wife of the ruler of the Maya site of Yaxchilan, consisted of a large collar with central medallion, matching cuffs and multi-part ear-flares, all presumably of green jade. Her complex head-dress includes deity insignia, sheathing elements probably of jade, and many trimmed feathers. Detail from Lintel 24 of Yaxchilan.

123 *Opposite* On this picture plaque of jade an important Maya ruler or noble sits on a throne wearing a bar pendant at this neck, an important belt mask at his waist, and ear, arm and ankle ornaments. A great head-dress is on his head and a square shield with a deity image is on one wrist. Before him is a dwarf wearing simpler ornaments.

LATIN AMERICAN INDIAN JEWELLERY

◆

124 Huichol beadwork, from San Andres Cohamiata, Jalisco, Mexico. These pieces are made as bracelets but may also be sewn to neck-collars and indicate their owner's wealth. Traditionally women's skills and craftsmanship expressed their devotion to their deities, and every motif had a sacred significance, such as the double-headed eagle, Tatei Werika Wimari, the sky spirit; the deer, Kauyumarie, the messenger god; geometric lines representing lightning or rain serpents; and flowers, the hearts of the gods.

The voraciousness of the Spanish Conquest in what is today Mexico and the Andean republics resulted in the large-scale destruction of Precolumbian works and the loss of indigenous arts. Where highly evolved and sophisticated techniques could be redirected to produce materials required by the Spanish they received a new stimulus, but with the suppression of traditional religion and the dissolution of the Indian élites which formed their main market, many of the arts and techniques not valued by the Spanish were lost.

As with other objects, traditional techniques for the production of jewellery survived in those areas least affected by Spanish colonisation. In less isolated regions new materials such as metals or ivory were incorporated and older techniques replaced. The working of jade in Mexico and bone-carving were abandoned shortly after the conquest. Contemporary jewellery made by the native peoples of Latin America makes use of locally available natural materials – feathers, skin, bone and minerals – as well as imported goods acquired by trade, such as beads, metals, mirrors, and other trinkets. Traditionally all of these materials had a symbolic significance within each culture. Among the Kayapó on the southern borders of the Amazon, for example, rock-crystal symbolises old age and the transcendence of social divisions and its use is reserved for senior men. It is regarded as their most precious possession, and lip-plugs of crystal are kept as family heirlooms. Feathers, too, are attributed supernatural powers by many of the Amazonian tribes and their use in head-dresses indicates the age, status and ethnic identity of the wearer. Recently, with the erosion of the automony or, indeed, the near extinction of many such cultures, and with the growth in craft production for the national and international tourist market, these unique associations are being lost.

The traditional excellence of Amazonian featherwork has led connoisseurs to refer to it as 'feather jewellery', and its decorative use has had a strong influence on European fashions since the seventeenth century. Feathers can be used in a variety of ways for ornament. The Bororo prefer to use long feathers with elaborate combinations of other materials and the Munduruku make loose arrangements of small feathers to produce crowns, while other tribes simply glue them onto their head and bodies or insert them into their pierced ear-lobes or nose. The versatility of feathers allows them to be made

125 Head-dress made of feathers
and jaguar pelt worn by elders of
the Ayoreode people, from
Zapaco, Bolivia. Fundamentalist
missionaries have destroyed much
of the traditional Ayoreode culture
and social organisation, and so
examples of their ornamental arts
are now seldom encountered.

into head-dresses, dorsal ornaments, armbands, necklaces and to be attached to belts
and labrets. Particular kinds of feather ornament are reserved for the two sexes, with men
exercising a near monopoly over the techniques of their construction in many societies.
The occasions when feathers are worn may also be restricted: the feather diadems of the
Umatina, on the borders of Brazil and Paraguay, are worn when making arrows, and at
funerals, and the Bororo use a special feather diadem to represent the dead, while the
Kayapó reserve the use of elaborate feather head-dresses for initiation ceremonies,
where they are associated with the name given to the initiate.

There are two main techniques for making feather ornaments. Long feathers may be
attached to rigid frames to produce large and elegant constructions, such as with the
diadems used by the Bororo, Karajá, Tapirapé, Kayapó and some northern Amazon
tribes, including the Apalai, Galibi and Waiwai. The second tradition practised by
Tupi-speaking peoples is to arrange smaller feathers on flexible frames to make necklaces, belts, crowns and even diadems. Some tribes such as the Tukano combine both
these techniques. Other forms of self adornment among the peoples of the Amazon
include the wearing of ear ornaments and lip-plugs. As we have already seen (Introduction), the decoration of the ear or mouth can relate to concepts about speech and hearing
within a culture. Among the Kayapó, for example, these ornaments are related to ideas

126 Woman's feather pendant
from the Gurupi River area,
Maranhâo, Brazil. The
Urubu-kaapor people have
preserved featherworking
techniques of the coastal Tupi from
pre-Conquest times. Particular
types of ornaments are restricted
to each of the sexes.

about knowledge and understanding. The size of a lip-plug indicates the oral assertive-
ness of its wearer and hence his status within a society placing high value on oratorical
skills. The piercing of ears is connected with the ability to hear and understand speech.
The ear-lobes of all infants are pierced and large cigar-shaped plugs inserted to ensure
that they develop this faculty. Once the child has learned to speak, the plug is replaced by
a string of beads.

Beads were introduced from Europe early in the conquest of America. Cortés traded
green glass beads, resembling precious jade, for gold in Mexico. Diverse tropical forest
groups in northern Pará have used beaded aprons since the eighteenth century.
However, in more accessible areas in the highlands and coastal regions bead-working
was taken up earlier and the technique developed to adapt them to indigenous ornaments. Among the Araucanians of Chile, European beads soon replaced the use of
polished malachite and azurite and sea-shells in the necklaces of women.

Beads are used in association with other materials throughout the Amazon region in
making adornments, but particularly fine examples are made by the Campa on the
Peruvian border and extravagant displays of beaded necklaces are worn by Panare
124 women. However, some of the most sumptuous and appealing beaded jewellery is made
by the Huichol, an isolated group in the northernmost area of the state of Jalisco in

Mexico. Huichol women make bead bracelets, necklaces, pendants and finger-rings for
use by both sexes. Other decorations such as anklets are now rarely used, while new
items such as elaborate belts with attached pendants modelled on similar embroidered
material in indigenous use are made for sale to commercial outlets. Three periods in the
development of the art can be distinguished: before 1910 when opaque beads were used
with colours largely limited to white, blue and red, an interim period distinguished by
the use of translucent beads, probably imported from Czechoslovakia, and the post-War
period, in which cheaper opaque European beads of many colours have been used. All
the motifs have a sacred significance and the patterns are thought to have been given to
the Huichol artists by tutelary deities. Some of the patterns are derived from the
markings on snakes, while others show their gods in animal forms or represent sacred
plants and flowers. The reproduction of the designs in beadwork indicates the religious
devotion of the women, and collars of threaded beads and necklaces with many beaded
bracelets attached to them are worn during ceremonial occasions, when they also
represent their owners' wealth.

Metal ornaments are most common in the areas more accessible to Western influence
and more closely resemble what we would recognise as jewellery in the West. The
Araucanians in Chile and the peoples of highland Bolivia, Ecuador and Peru have a long
established metalworking tradition which predates the Spanish Conquest. The earliest
recorded metal ornaments were large, circular and quadrangular ear pendants worn by

Araucanian headmen, but most of these metal objects were reserved for the decoration of saddles and riding equipment. In the nineteenth century the number of pectorals, pendants, headbands, necklaces, bracelets, anklets and rings worn by Araucanian women greatly increased, as in other parts of South America. The characteristic forms of this articulated metal jewellery, which had crosses, discs and figures suspended from the main metal sheets, has assumed increasingly complex designs.

In the Andes the single most characteristic ornament is the *tapu*, a long pin surmounted ₁₂₇ by a spherical or spoon-like decoration which is used by the women to fasten their cloaks. Silver rings and necklaces made from coins threaded with beads are also commonly used to indicated the wealth and position of their wearers. The designs on silver coinage sometimes have a special importance to the indigenous culture which adds to their attraction. The contemporary descendants of the Maya in Guatemala use silver rings in marriage ceremonies and in some areas women still have long necklaces of small decorated silver spheres which form part of their inherited wealth.

Despite almost five hundred years of traumatic upheavals Amerindians have been partly successful in domesticating foreign ideas, tastes and materials to their own world vision, but the increasingly predatory globalisation of local markets now seriously threatens this delicate and shifting equilibrium and with it the traditional sense of ornamental art.

128 Silver pins or *tapus* of the Quechua/Aymara, Andes area of Peru or Bolivia. These examples are decorated with bird and animal figures, carved blue glass inlays and pendants. They are of a less common type than those with spoon-shaped ends (see illustration opposite contents page). Like 127, these pins would have been used to fasten women's cloaks.

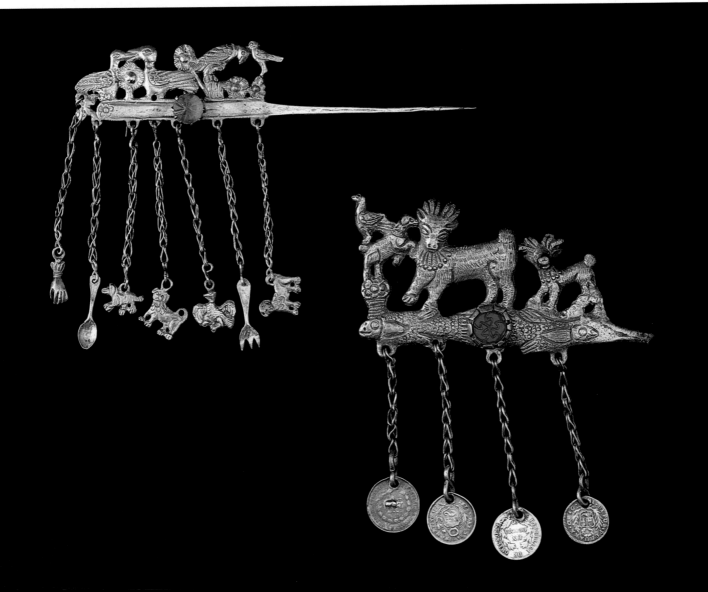

NORTH AMERICAN
INDIAN JEWELLERY

◆

129 Crow Indian, Northern Plains, photographed in the 1870s, wearing silver hoop ear-rings, probably strung with silver beads, a style later adopted by the Navajo in the South-west. The white discs attached to his elaborate necklace were cut from buffalo shoulder plates.

Early European travellers in North America have left vivid, often beautiful descriptions of the finery worn by the Indians whom they encountered. While such descriptions tend to reflect their writers' fascination with the exotic as well as, perhaps, their imagination, personal ornament and body decoration were nevertheless significant elements in Indian culture. The wearing of jewellery was also a demonstration of wealth and status, both conspicuous and implied. Among the nineteenth-century Omaha, for example, ear-piercing was a costly ceremony, each hole representing the gift of a horse to the man who did the piercing. Thus Omaha ear ornaments were doubly indicative of their wearers' wealth.

In the prehistoric period (that is, prior to European contact) beads, ear-plugs and breast ornaments were laboriously cut from stone. Often a particularly striking material was chosen, such as alabaster, nephrite or banded slate, ground smooth on a sandstone block and polished to a high lustre. Excavations at the great Anasazi site of Pueblo Bonito have recovered some spectacular items of prehistoric jewellery, perhaps the most notable being a four-strand necklace of over two thousand graduated beads of polished blue turquoise.

Gorgets or breast ornaments were also cut from bone, usually animal, occasionally human, and decorated with engraved or painted designs. Smaller hollow bones, like those of birds, required little effort to transform them into tubular beads, and along both the Pacific and Atlantic coasts fish vertebrae were strung together as necklaces and bracelets or as spacers between other types of beads. In the South-west hair ornaments were made, consisting of bone points tied together to form combs and topped with tufts of feathers.

Both shell and copper were widely used for making necklaces, bracelets, ear ornaments and pendants. Small shells were utilised as beads by simply grinding off the ends to make it possible to string them. Larger shells were cut into breast ornaments of various forms or in cross-section to make bracelets. They were also cut and ground into small flat discs which could then be easily drilled for stringing as beads.

Raw copper, extracted from surface outcrops or shallow pits, was worked into the required shape or beaten into thin sheets by alternate cold-hammering and annealing.

130 *Right* Pomo woman's ear-plug from California, made of an engraved bird bone and a basketry disc decorated with shell and glass beads. Although no trace now remains, the basketry may originally have been covered with feathers.

131 *Opposite* Ottawa body ornament, Great Lakes region, consisting of a shell gorget and two back panels of porcupine quillwork. The panels are linked by two shoulder straps of glass beads in imitation of wampum. The design of the quillwork depicts the mythical Thunderbird.

The techniques of smelting and casting were unknown in aboriginal North America. That copper was regarded in the pre-contact period as a rare and precious material is suggested by the fact that the majority of surviving objects made of this metal are items of jewellery – head- and breastplates, ear and hair ornaments, bracelets and anklets.

Perhaps the most remarkable feature concerning the use of shell and copper, however, is the distribution of both the raw material and the finished products. Marine shells, for example, which could only have come from the coast of southern California, have been excavated as far north as south-west Colorado and as far east as Texas. In the case of copper, the largest deposits lie on the southern shores of Lake Superior, with lesser deposits in the Appalachian Mountains and along the Atlantic coast. From these sources the raw metal and the objects made from it were carried many hundreds of miles to the south and east. In the South-west copper artefacts were imported from Mexico and shells

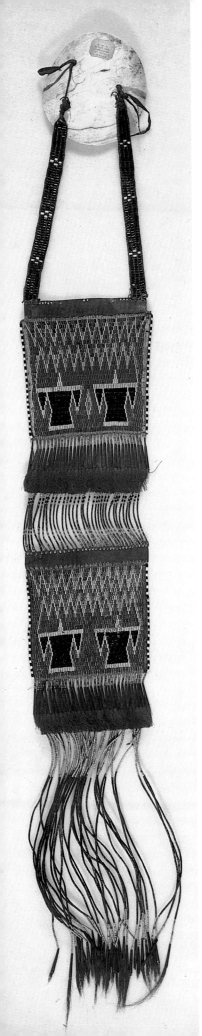

from the Gulf of Mexico and the Californian coast. What the evidence in fact suggests is the existence of vast and complex trading networks in operation perhaps as early as 5000 BC. Just how extensive were these trading networks is exemplified by the richness of the grave goods excavated from the burial mounds of the Hopewell people, whose culture flourished in the Ohio Valley from around 100 BC to AD 300. The Hopewell Indians were farmers, traders and artists of exceptional ability. Within their burial mounds the bones of the dead were surrounded with great quantities of jewellery made of pearl, copper and silver, shell and animal teeth.

The function of prehistoric jewellery is not always apparent from its form, but the manner of wear can often be deduced from its disposition within a grave. Bracelets may yet encircle an armbone, for example, or ear-spools flank a skull. Information about clothing and ornament can also be gained from other types of burial offerings, such as figurines, human effigy vessels, or depictions engraved on bone or shell, or on cut sheets of copper or mica. It is clear that societies such as that of the Hopewell were complex and highly organised. Burials were probably accompanied by elaborate ceremonies. The buried dead would have been people of wealth and high status, and the objects interred with them would almost certainly have had ceremonial value and importance in accordance with that status. Thus, to treat and discuss such objects as simple jewellery, and in terms only of their decorative function, is probably a gross oversimplification. However, their ritual significance remains something about which we can only speculate.

With the coming of Europeans and the appearance of written sources, much more information about Indian personal decoration and jewellery becomes available, although it is not always in a reliable form and there is still room for discussion concerning distinctions between ceremonial regalia and simple jewellery.

Copper continued to be used in the historic period until displaced in popularity by brass and silver during the course of the eighteenth century. With the exception of the Arctic, where stone labrets continued to be worn until the end of the nineteenth century, and of the South-west, where the use of semi-precious stones and minerals still flourishes, stone was not much utilised for ornament in the historic period. There is, however, one reference to a stone ornament which is particularly interesting, although not by reason of the material. According to Antoine de la Mothe Cadillac, writing of the Ottawa Indians in 1695: 'the word Ottawa means Nation of the Pierced Noses because they pierce their noses and attach to the nose a small prettily ornamented stone which comes to the middle of the mouth between the lips. It is a fashion with them, they would not think themselves properly decked out if that were wanting. There are nevertheless, some old men who maintain that it is a protection against medicine, that is to say, against the fates and spells that their enemies and other malicious persons might cast on them to poison them and make them die.'

The idea that a piece of jewellery might have been for its owner more than a decorative device would probably have been well understood by our early commentators, since similar ideas also pertained in Europe. Pearls, obtained from freshwater mussels, certainly seem to have been used ceremonially. In 1540 Hernando de Soto's expedition to conquer and settle the South-east found a temple or mortuary house on the Savannah River where pearls covered the bodies of the dead in such profusion that his troops carried away a quantity variously estimated as being between 165 and 350 pounds in weight. The early eighteenth-century French traveller Pénicaut claimed that a sacred pearl necklace was kept in the Natchez temple and that two or three pearls were tied around the necks of highborn Natchez infants, who wore these until they were ten years old, when the pearls were returned to the temple. When worn as jewellery, pearls, like copper, were clearly indicative of high social status. The 'chieftainess' who welcomed de

132 Necklace from the Plains region. Grizzly bear claws are strung on cord with glass bead spacers and a copper cross pendant. Such necklaces were highly prized, since they implied hunting prowess and so conferred considerable distinction on their wearers.

Soto to the town of Cofitachequi ceremonially presented him with a many-stringed pearl necklace which she took from around her own neck.

The use of pearls does not appear to have survived European colonisation of the South-east. Clearly, as witnessed by de Soto's looting of the temple, Europeans found them highly desirable, probably much more so than bone or copper, and it may be, therefore, that early written sources give pearls undue importance. The Indians' method of extracting the pearls from their shells and of drilling them for stringing involved the application of heat, which caused discoloration. These processes are often commented upon by early writers with no small degree of vexation, since the pearls were thus spoiled for commercial purposes.

Even with the increasing influx of European goods and materials, Indians continued to

130 make use of local plants and animals. In the South-west prehistoric sites have yielded up beads made from seeds, berries and acorn cups, and in the same area today the tradition persists, with necklaces being made of brightly dyed maize kernels, seeds and nuts. In the early nineteenth century the explorers Lewis and Clark noted a collar of quilled, twisted grass worn by a Shoshone, and necklaces of sweet-smelling roots were found among the Mandan and Blackfoot. (Perhaps, like the braids of sweetgrass worn by Omaha men under their shirts, these were worn more as perfumery than as decoration.) On the North-west Coast Haida, Tlingit and Tsimshian women of rank wore elliptical wooden labrets inserted through their lower lips.

Several early writers mention the prevalence of bird and animal claws as head and ear 132 decoration. In the Plains area grizzly bear claws were widely used for necklaces, strung on cords or on lengths of folded skin, fur or cloth. The Crow decorated their bear-claw 129 necklaces with discs cut from buffalo shoulder blades, polished and whitened with clay. So highly prized were bear claws that, as the grizzly bear population declined during the latter part of the nineteenth century, an increasing number of imitation claws were 133 carved from horn, hoof, wood and, latterly, synthetic materials.

Strips of skin and fur, occasionally entire animal feet or paws, were also worn. Chokers of otter fur, with or without attached bear claws, were popular wear in the eastern Plains area, and, on the North-west Coast, young Kwakiutl and Nootka women wore bracelets and anklets of sea-otter fur.

Deer hooves and dewclaws, and the teeth of bears, rodents, buffalo, deer and elk were used both to decorate items of clothing and as necklaces and pendants. Elk teeth in particular were so highly prized that imitations were carved from bone. On the North- 138 west Coast and in the Arctic walrus ivory was used for labrets and beads.

At least until the end of the eighteenth century, horn and antler were used in some 135 areas to make armbands and bracelets. The Coast Salish, for example, formed bracelets 134 from strips of mountain-goat horn, bent into loops and incised with curvilinear motifs. The method of working antler and bone was probably similar to that described by Du Pratz for the manufacture of bone bracelets in the early eighteenth century on the lower Mississippi. There young men sometimes 'put on bracelets made of the ribs of deer which they have worked down very thin and bent in boiling water. These bracelets are as white and smooth as polished ivory outside.'

Shell beads receive frequent mention in the early literature, due largely to the fact that they acted as a medium of currency and ceremonial exchange. Thus Francis Louis Michel, referring to the use of shell money in Virginia around 1700, writes: 'They [the Indians] do not esteem silver or gold, and do not want to take it. Their money is like the material they hang around them, but small, of white and pearly color, like small corals, strung on a string. It is sold by the yard so to speak. They measure from the index finger to the elbow, which length costs half an English crown.'

The acquisition of metal tools led to the large-scale manufacture of the cylindrical beads of white and purple clamshell commonly known as 'wampum', but the native product was very quickly displaced by wampum of European make, including glass imitations, and oversupply eventually led to its becoming worthless, at least as currency. However, the term 'wampum' continued to be applied to clamshell beads made for the Indian trade by European settlers. (The Dutch settlements in New Jersey seem to have had a monopoly here, at least in the colonial period.) Later the term also came to be attached to other forms of shell ornament made by whites, such as shell gorgets or 'wampum moons' and the long tubular beads popularly known as 'hair pipes'. These last illustrate how European trade goods included not only new materials and forms, but also modified or substituted versions of aboriginal prototypes.

133 Blackfoot necklace, Northern Plains, of imitation bear claws carved from cow-horn. The undersides of genuine bear claws were sometimes painted red and this has also been copied. Today plastic and bone imitations attest to the necklaces' continuing popularity.

Archaeological evidence has shown that tubular beads of stone, bone, shell and copper were used in the prehistoric period for necklaces and as ear and hair ornaments. Long shell beads, made from the central column of the marine conch, are mentioned by several writers in the colonial period. Du Pratz, for example, refers to 'earrings made of the core of a great shell called "burgo" . . . This ear pendant is as large as the little finger and at least as long.' James Adair, in his *History of the American Indians*, published in 1775, describes the use of wampum among the Cherokees, Creeks and Chickasaw, and goes on: 'Formerly four deer-skins was the price of a large conch-shell bead about the length and thickness of a man's fore-finger; which they fixed to the crown of their head, as an high ornament – so greatly they valued them.' (Hence the designation of this type of ornament by white traders as a 'wampum hair pipe'.)

The manufacture of shell hair pipes by white settlers probably began sometime during the 1770s and continued well into the second half of the nineteenth century. Although they were used by some Woodlands and South-western groups, hair pipes tend to be most frequently associated with the Plains area, where they were worn in the form of necklaces, as hair ornaments suspended on cords on either side of the head and as ear pendants. As hair and ear decoration, they seem to have been worn more commonly by men.

The mechanisation, at some point in the 1850s, of the drilling process, hitherto done laboriously by hand, and the resultant increase in output led not only to the more widespread use of hair pipes, but also to greater elaboration in the objects made from them. The most striking example of this was the development of the so-called breastplate worn by many of the Plains tribes from the 1850s onwards. This ornament, hung around the neck, consisted of a large number of hair pipes strung horizontally or diagonally on buckskin cords in two or more vertical rows. A further boost to the development of the 136 breastplate was given by the appearance of bone hair pipes in the 1880s. Made from the leg-bones of cattle, they were cheaper to produce and less fragile, and their use rapidly superseded that of shell hair pipes.

134 Bracelets of mountain goat horn of the Coast Salish, North-west Coast (late 18th century). They were made by softening the horn in boiling water so that it could be bent into loops. The incised designs may originally have contained some form of inlay and one bracelet still has a white glass bead attached.

The hair pipe necklace also developed a more complex form, particularly in the northern Plains in the Reservation period, with the several strands of the necklace passing around the neck, then joining about waist level to form a panel or series of panels of vertically arranged hair pipes, often alternating with panels of glass beads, and reaching almost to the wearer's feet. Although sometimes described as a woman's ornament, this type of necklace was in fact worn by both men and women. The breastplate, on the other hand, was worn exclusively by men. The fashion for hair pipes as hair ornaments, incidentally, seems to have become obsolete in the 1880s.

Closely rivalling hair pipes in popularity, and in some areas preferred, were dentalia or 137 tooth shells. Obtained principally on the west coast of Vancouver Island, they were widely traded and used as a medium of currency. At European contact they were found in use from northern California to the Arctic as far east as the Mackenzie Delta, and on the northern Plains as far east as the village tribes of the Upper Missouri. As currency, they were carefully graded by size and evaluated accordingly. The fur traders Alexander Henry and David Thompson noted the trade in dentalia in 1813: 'The best quality are two inches long. One fathom [six feet] of these shells is valued at three blankets of two and a

135 *Left* Bent antler armband from the North-east Woodlands, incised and decorated with deer-hair tassels. It was fastened by means of thongs passing through holes drilled for the purpose. The silver armbands introduced by the fur traders appear to have been copied directly from such prototypes.

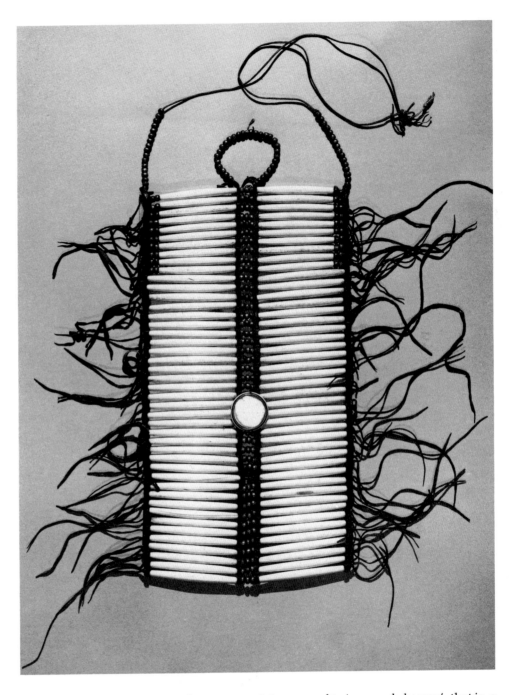

136 *Right* Sioux man's breastplate, Northern Plains (late 19th century). It consists of two rows of bone hair pipes separated by brass beads and leather strips, with a small round mirror in the centre. All the components would have been supplied by traders.

half points . . .' (In trading parlance, one point was equal to 'one made beaver', that is, a stretched and dried beaver pelt.)

Dentalia were distributed both by white traders, who named the shells 'Iroquois beads', and also through intertribal trade. Edwin Thompson Denig described how this trade operated in the 1850s in relation to the Assiniboin on the Upper Missouri. This shell, he wrote, 'is sought after by them [the Indians] more eagerly than anything else of the kind. They are procured on the coast of the Pacific and find their way to our tribes across the mountains through the different nations by traffic with each other until the Crows and Blackfeet get them from some bands of the Snake and Flathead Indians with whom they are at peace.' Dentalium shell breastplates were worn by the Dakota until replaced by those made of hair pipes. More widely the shells were worn in the form of

137 *Above* Skin headband from the North-west Coast, decorated with rows of dentalium shells and glass beads. Dentalia were valued not only for their ornamental qualities, but also as the principal currency unit of the area.

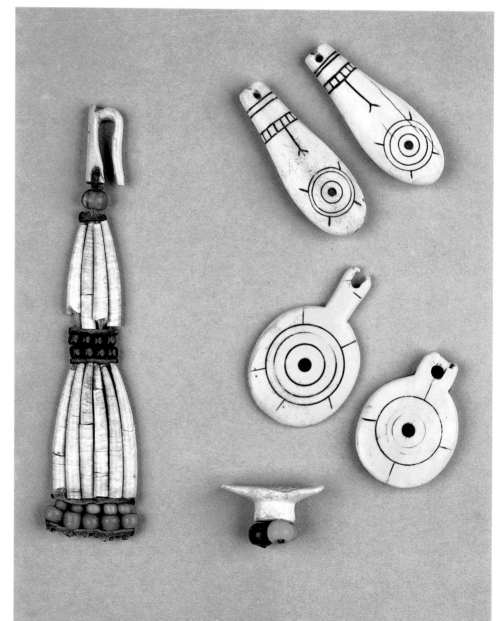

138 *Right* Western Eskimo ear-rings and labret. On the left, a woman's ear-ring consisting of a walrus ivory hook hung with dentalia and blue glass beads. On the right (*top and centre*), women's ear-rings of incised walrus ivory. At the bottom, a man's ivory labret decorated with blue glass beads; such items were worn on either side of the lower lip.

chokers, loop necklaces and ear-pendants. The Nez Percé wore them as nose ornaments, transversely through the nasal septum.

Abalone shells were also imported into the Plains from the Pacific coast, although, according to Denig, they were by his time rather less valuable than previously, owing to oversupply by traders. On the Plains and along the Pacific coast itself, cut pieces of abalone were formed into necklaces and ear-pendants, sometimes in conjunction with dentalia. The value placed on this shell is indicated by the use of abalone shell necklaces by the Californian Indians as offerings to the dead at their annual mourning ceremonies. A journalist, Stephen Powers, who witnessed a ceremony of this type in the 1870s, has

139 Slow Bull's wife, a Sioux woman photographed by Edward Curtis *c*. 1900. Her necklace, bandolier and hair ornaments are composed of bone hair pipes and her ear-pendants are of dentalia and abalone (*Haliotis*) shell. Dentalia also decorate her dress.

left a vivid and dramatic account of 'glittering necklaces' of abalone shell being held high over the heads of the dancers.

As well as supplying traditional materials or imitations of them, European traders also introduced a whole range of new materials. The variety of goods offered, firstly through gift-giving ceremonies to secure alliance and friendship, then through the fur trade, had a radical effect, supplementing and often replacing native equivalents. As the pace of trade increased, so more and more goods were brought on to the market by merchants anxious to win Indian custom and furs. By the 1850s the 'great variety of trinkets . . . furnished by the traders' included 'brass rings, brass and iron wire, beads, brass hair and breast plates, brass and silver gorgets, wampum moons, hair pipes, St Lawrence shells, spotted seashells, hawk bells, horse and sleigh bells, cock and ostrich feathers, thimbles, gold and silver lace, etc.' The bulk of these items, including the bells and thimbles, were supplied to the Indians as jewellery materials, and were indeed used as such by them.

Perhaps the most common and enduring of all trade items were glass beads. These had been among the items offered by Christopher Columbus to the Indians who greeted him when he landed in the Bahamas in October 1492. Later explorers and traders followed suit. In 1603 when Martin Pring left Bristol for Virginia, 'furnished with slight merchandizes thought fit to trade with the people of the Countrey', his cargo included 'Bels, Beades, Bugles . . . and such like.'

The beads carried by Martin Pring would almost certainly have been made in Venice, the principal centre of glass manufacture in Europe until its decline in the late eighteenth century. The earliest beads introduced tended to be large (over ¼ inch in diameter) and

140 Necklace of white glass beads and pendants cut from the inner mother-of-pearl surface of the abalone shell, from California.

either round or cylindrical, the latter being known as 'bugles' or 'rods'. Blue and white seem to have been the most common colours, but there was also a two-coloured variety, with a red exterior and a white or dark-green interior. A number of cylindrical beads of unusual length (some almost 6 inches long) have been found in close association with skulls in Susquehanna burials of the 1640s, and it has been suggested that these may have been specifically manufactured as glass substitutes for native-made shell hair pipes. Presumably because of their fragility, they do not appear to have become popular.

Other forms of glass bead, however, were readily accepted and gradually came to replace beads made of materials such as shell and bone for the making of necklaces, 141 bracelets, ear-pendants and so on. At first used sparingly, and confined to the Atlantic and Pacific coastal areas where they were introduced, glass beads came to be found well away from the main trade routes. In 1778 Captain Cook found the Inuit of north-west Alaska in possession of glass beads, some of which they wore hanging from their ears.

By the early years of the nineteenth century, glass beads had been traded into the Plains area. Early nineteenth-century beads, known as 'pony beads' or 'pound beads', were smaller than the earlier type, and the 1830s saw the appearance of the even smaller 'seed bead'. Both these types of bead tended in the main to be applied directly to clothing in the form of embroidery, but various items of jewellery were also made. Some Plains tribes wore close-fitting chokers, consisting of two rolls of buckskin, wrapped round with strings of beads, and tied around the wearer's neck with buckskin thongs. Another type of necklace, popular in the northern Plains, was the loop necklace, composed of several bead-wrapped hide loops (perhaps ten or twelve) suspended from long strips of leather. The whole was hung around the neck on a thong. In the Eastern Woodlands strips of woven beadwork, often of intricate design, were worn as necklets, headbands, armbands, belts and garters.

By the end of the nineteenth century glass beads were widely available in many colours, shapes and sizes, and were used in great quantity and with much imagination. In north-west Alaska, for example, an ornament worn by both men and women 142 consisted of several strings of beads suspended from the wearer's ear-plugs and looped under the chin. For sheer profusion, however, it is difficult to better the following description of a young Seminole woman in the 1880s: 'She was the proud wearer of certainly not fewer than two hundred strings of good sized beads. She had six quarts [probably a peck of the beads] gathered about her neck, hanging down her back, down upon her breasts, filling the space under her chin and covering her neck up to her ears. It was an effort for her to move her head.'

Yet not everywhere were glass beads readily accepted, as Captain Cook found when he visited the North-west Coast in 1778. There the Indians had no interest in beads, only in metal and that avidly: 'Nothing would go down with our visitors but metal . . . Whole suits of clothes were stripped of every button; bureaus of their furniture, and copper kettles, tin canisters, candlesticks and the like, all went to wreck.' While much of the metalwork thus acquired would have gone towards the making of tools and weapons, some items at least were utilised as jewellery. The adoption of European metal objects as items of jewellery began early. Cartier presented tin buttons and bells to the Huron in the 1530s and half a century later Arthur Barlowe described a North Carolina Indian wearing a tin dish as a breastplate. By the nineteenth century, as well as bells and buttons, coins, curtain rings, thimbles and cartridge cases, lengths of fine chain and small mirrors were also being used as decorative components or attachments.

Ready-made items of jewellery were also supplied. The trade goods carried by Lewis and Clark in 1804, for example, included rings (described as 'cheap, ornamented with colored glass or mockstone'), iron and brass combs, silver arm- and wristbands,

141 *Above* Naskapi girls' ear
ornaments, Eastern Subarctic,
consisting of glass beadwork
stitched to a cloth backing and
attached to the ears by means of
ribbons. The materials were
probably supplied by the
Hudson's Bay Company.

142 *Right* Kenowun, an Eskimo
woman from Nunivak Island,
Alaska, photographed by Edward
Curtis in 1928. She wears
nose-beads and a pair of beaded
ivory labrets in her lower lip. Her
ivory ear ornaments are connected
by strings of beads passing under
her chin.

ear-rings, nose trinkets and brooches. A high proportion were probably of base metal
and, in general, the type of metal offered seems to have made little difference, brass,
copper, iron, tin and silver being equally acceptable to the Indians.

In the Eastern Woodlands area, however, around the Great Lakes and the Upper
Mississippi and along the Atlantic coast, a taste for silver jewellery predominated.
Originally introduced in the form of diplomatic largesse, silver became a popular item in
commercial trade, and by the mid-eighteenth century large quantities of silver ornaments
were produced, both in Europe and in North America, specifically for trade with the
Indians. Some of these ornaments, such as armbands and circular gorgets, were clearly
derived from aboriginal prototypes of bone and shell, but others were of European form
and design. Brooches, for example, in the form of Masonic emblems, were much
favoured by the Iroquois, although they attached no Masonic significance to them.

Indeed, brooches of various shapes were among the most popular silver ornaments,
and Iroquois women in particular wore large numbers pinned to their clothing, both back
and front. Men also wore them as hair ornaments, together with disc-shaped hair-plates

and tubular hair pipes. Ear-pendants were worn by both men and women, as well as finger-rings and nose-rings. Bracelets and bands for arm, leg and head were made of strips of sheet silver of varying widths, with holes drilled at the ends for ties. Headbands, sometimes two or three at one time, were often incorporated into head-dresses or used to trim European hats. Along with circular or crescent gorgets, these were worn by tribal leaders as marks of rank.

The decline of the fur trade in the early nineteenth century led to the virtual cessation in the supply of trade silver. By this time, however, some of the Indians had acquired silversmithing skills for themselves, so that silver continued to be a customary element in Woodland Indian costume and ceremonial, at least until the end of the century. A little trade silver reached the Plains from the Eastern Indians as well as from Spanish settlements in New Mexico and, by the early years of the nineteenth century, Plains Indians, like the Iroquois, were beginning to wear metal jewellery of their own making. Such jewellery (bracelets of brass or copper wire, for example) remained comparatively rare until the 1860s when traders introduced the so-called German silver, an alloy of nickel, zinc and copper. For the next twenty years or so Plains metalwork flourished and distinctive styles of ornament emerged, particularly among the Indians of the southern Plains. Graduated sets of delicately engraved hair-plates, sometimes twenty or more, were attached directly to long hair queues or to hair-pieces consisting of lengths of horsehair, cloth or leather. Breast ornaments were also made, their scalloped, crescentic and cruciform shapes pointing to Spanish influence. Plains metalworking, unfortunately, contained the seeds of its own decline, for, with the ready availability of metal ornaments, their prestige value diminished and, by the 1880s, they were no longer in favour.

The most remarkable and perhaps best-known development of Indian silverwork
143 occurred in the South-west, particularly among the Navajo. Evidence suggests that Navajo had worn silver jewellery since the late sixteenth century, obtained successively from Spanish, Mexican and Plains Indian sources. By the 1840s they had begun to work in metal, making brass bracelets and ear-rings from wire supplied by traders. When they first began to work in silver is not entirely clear, but in 1864 a New Mexico newspaper was able to report that the Navajo 'manufacture silver ornaments of a very creditable style of workmanship'. These early ornaments closely followed the pattern of those traded from the Spanish and the Plains Indians. Belt decorations, for example, consisted of small round or oval plates called conchas (from the Spanish word meaning shell), similar to and probably deriving from hair-plates.

By the 1880s the Navajo had added necklaces, bracelets and rings to their repertoire and had begun to set stones in silver. Turquoise was always preferred, but other stones were also used, and contemporary writers mention garnet, agate, malachite, jasper and cornelian, among others. A recognisable Navajo style began to develop, one of the most distinctive items to emerge being the so-called 'squash blossom' necklace, composed of flower-like silver beads, which are probably derived from Spanish beads in the form of pomegranates. This necklace usually incorporates a central *naja*, a crescent-shaped pendant, again of Spanish origin and also used on the Plains.

Following Navajo example, some of the Pueblo groups also began to work in silver towards the end of the nineteenth century and developed distinctive styles of their own. Zuni jewellery, for example, is characterised by the setting of turquoise, coral, shell and jet in intricate mosaic patterns.

During the early years of the twentieth century traders encouraged the Indians to produce jewellery specifically for the growing tourist market in the south-west, providing them with sheet silver and pre-cut stones, as well as suggesting new forms and

143 Silver bracelets of the Navajo, South-west, *c.* 1940, set with turquoise. The left-hand bracelet, of three wires, has stamped decoration, as does the centre one; the right-hand bracelet, also of three wires, has applied 'teardrop' decoration. Traders would have supplied both the wire and the sheet silver.

motifs. By 1930 the tourist market had become predominant and, although many smiths continued to work in the traditional way, much of the jewellery made then (and even still today) is in the form of cheap, commercially mass-produced 'railroad curios'.

The formation of Indian craft guilds and the establishment of competitions to promote good design and craftsmanship have gone some way towards reversing this trend. Across North America, on the North-west Coast, in the Woodlands, the Plains and the South-west, Indian artists are making conscious efforts to blend tradition with originality and innovation. Nowhere, perhaps, is this more clearly demonstrated than in the South-west, where contemporary silversmiths, including those from other areas, have drawn on early jewellery styles to produce work which is vigorous, sophisticated and highly individualistic. The use of gold as well as silver has led to a refinement of metalworking techniques and new skills have been developed in the setting of stones, not only turquoise, although that remains most popular, but also diamonds, pearls, opals, lapis lazuli from Afghanistan, charoite from Siberia, lavulite from the Kalahari Desert. Individual artists like Harvey Begay, Ted Charveze, Raymond Yazzie, Richard Tsosie (all Navajo), Charles Loloma (Hopi) and Ben Nighthorse (Cheyenne) have come to prominence as artists in their own right. Their work is found in art galleries, not in craft shops, and commands high prices. While it is true that their market, like that of the curio shops, is predominantly non-Indian, it is one which they supply on their own terms and to which they make no concessions.

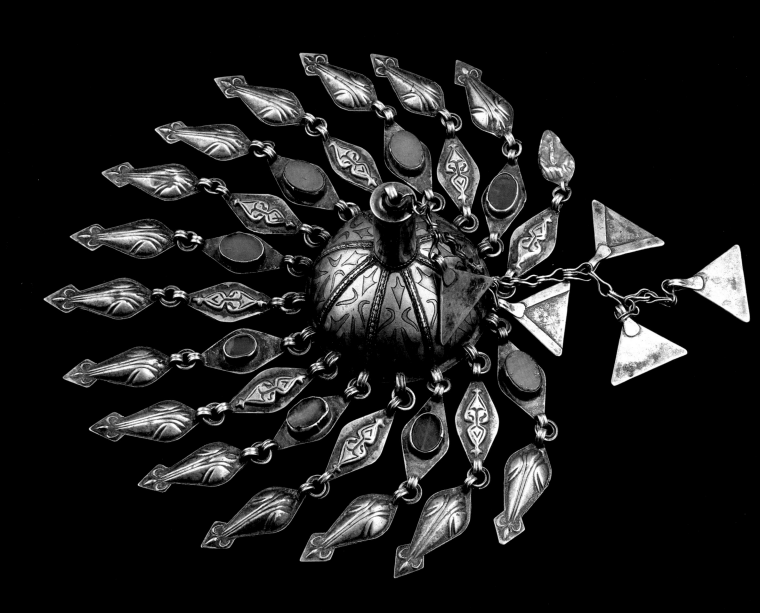

6

Materials and techniques

♦

144 A girl's hat ornament (*doğācik*) from Russian Turkestan (Yumat Türkmeny, late 19th century). It is made of silver with gilt arabesques; its central domed finial has radiating chains with pendants set with cornelians.

When we look at the ethnic jewellery produced by the people of South America, Africa, North America, the Middle East, India, the Far East and the Pacific we are at times struck by a certain indefinable similarity evident in some of this work. One wonders what can account for this impression when these cultures are so widely dispersed geographically, and each is liable to be distinct in character. Is there perhaps some underlying feature common to these objects, no matter how far their creators were separated in time and place? There is an answer, and it is technology.

An example can be seen in the striking similarity between beaded collars made by the Inuit of Greenland and necklaces made by Oraon women on the other side of the world in Bihar, India. The explanation lies in what is technically possible in stringing the kind of small seed beads used, and very similar systems have been exploited by both peoples for their assembly. Other examples can be given. In silver filigree jewellery, made in such places as Iceland, Norway, Portugal, Morocco and India, the medium is wire. For structural strength the process of construction requires a basic frame of heavier wire, within which lightweight filler wires are fixed. These common elements make all filigree objects part of the same technological family.

In various parts of the world metal jewellery has been made by the techniques of lost-wax casting (see p. 183). Wax, either in sheet form or in long, flexible threads, is used to make a model of the final object. Wax threads lend themselves to designs featuring circles and 'twisted' wire; wax sheets are used to create larger, more plainly modelled areas. A Precolumbian cast-gold pendant from Colombia, in the form of an eagle, illustrates the point: its border imitates twisted wire and incorporates openwork circles. A bronze pendant from Nagpur, India, offers an interesting comparison; although differing in the material used, actual form and in the details of its decoration, it also has a border with a similar design of twisted wire and openwork circles.

From these and many other possible examples we can conclude that technology and design are inseparable: faced with the same problems, craftsmen the world over have explored similar avenues in dealing with the technical limitations and possibilities presented by any particular material.

173

145, 146 *Right and below right* The
systems possible for stringing seed
beads can lead to similarities of
design in widely differing cultures.
An Oraon girl from Bihar, India
(145), dressed for a festival, wears
a seed bead collar-type necklace,
fringed with coloured cotton
pompons. A comparable method
of construction has been used for a
collar of seed beads on a cotton
shirt from Greenland (146),
producing a similar effect.

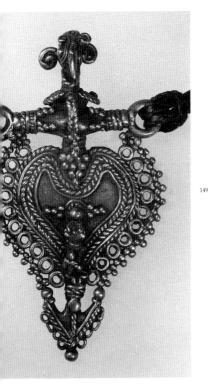

147, 148 *Above* A Precolumbian gold pendant from Sinú, Colombia (147, *above*) and a bronze pendant from Nagpur, India (148, *top*). Both of these lost-wax castings have similar borders of 'twisted wire' and circles created by the use of wax threads in the original model, while wax sheets have been used to create the more plainly modelled areas.

The raw materials

Adorning the body is a universal human activity; this book has shown the diversity of materials that even a single culture might exploit to produce a varied range of ornaments. Looking at the jewellery created in far-flung parts of the world, it would appear that in several cases a culture may display a decided preference for certain materials, although the choice may simply be dictated by what is available.

The local environment has always been an important source, and the kind of technological processes that have been explored in particular places can often be closely related to the character of the materials that are most readily available. The immediate surroundings might offer a variety of organic materials. Plants, an ancient source, contributed attractive materials which, though perishable, could with relatively little manipulation serve a temporary function, such as adornment during a religious festival or communal social event. Flowers and fibres of all kinds have been used in diverse ways which exploit their colour and form. The structural systems invented to hold them together include twining, braiding, tying, knotting, wrapping and stringing. Besides the use of actual flowers, they have also offered inspiration to craftsmen making jewellery from other materials, especially metals. Here they may perform not merely decorative functions, but may have broader cultural and symbolic dimensions.

Birds yielded an endless source of feathers and other materials, such as beaks and casques, especially from those unfortunate creatures whom nature has provided with the most colourful and lustrous plumage. An infinite number of techniques were invented for assembling ornaments of feathers, techniques such as stitching, appliqué, mosaic patterning, twining, and glueing.

The world of insects was not neglected as a resource, and, for instance, the iridescent *elytrae* or wing cases of a class of beetle (Buprestidae) were commonly used for their vibrant colour, as well as their durability.

Animals primarily provided mankind with nourishment, though hunting to eradicate local predatory animals also occurred. Some of the remains, such as skin, teeth, bones, ivory, tushes and horns were commonly used for decorative purposes, and still are, even though today the hunter is more often a sportsman than a provider. Rights to wear these objects may indicate prowess; the materials in this case are in part trophies. Beyond that, they may recall characteristics of the animal itself, which may act as an appropriate metaphor for the social position of the wearer.

Of the mineral materials, stone was the first to be used for implements that cut, scrape or bore, and for making arrow- and spear-heads. The use of stones suitable for tool-making entailed a detailed knowledge of various stone types. At an early date precious and semi-precious stones were used for decoration, mainly as beads; the first hardstone beads may have been made by piercing holes in pebbles. The use of these stones in a non-functional context suggests an interest in particular qualities in their colour, markings, degree of translucency or hardness, any of which put them in a special category. Beads ultimately came to have amuletic rather than purely decorative functions. Their durability – far greater than any other material except metal – may have given them a special value as objects to be passed on from generation to generation. Hardstone beads have been incorporated into jewellery by many of the peoples discussed in this book, and the different stones available locally or by trade can often strongly characterise the ornaments of a particular culture. To give but one example, Mongolian metal jewellery is distinguished by the liberal use of coral and turquoise beads.

Glass as a material for personal ornament came at a later date, with the development of glass technology. Initially its use was to replicate the rarer and more costly hardstones.

175

149 Necklaces from East and Southern Africa. The top necklace is made from scented wood and belongs to the Kikuyu tribe; the others, from the Fingo tribe, are of various types of seeds interspersed with glass beads.

Ancient Egyptian glass, and later Imperial Chinese glass was manufactured with the metallic oxides that would make the resulting colours resemble genuine cornelian, turquoise, lapis lazuli and, in China, jade – all highly valued in these cultures.

Today glass can be made in any colour, and it has developed a complex technology of its own. In some cases processes related to stone-working, such as carving and faceting, are still applied to glass. The basic and important difference between these materials is that because glass is viscous in its molten state, it can be moulded to any form, and it can be worked by additive methods, unlike stone whose technology is always subtractive.

Metal, of all mineral substances used for ornamentation, is of prime importance in many parts of the world. Practically all metals and many alloys, such as brass and bronze, have been used for jewellery, but especially favoured are the precious metals, gold and silver. Their relative rarity is what accounts for the designation 'precious', but equally important to the craftsman is their characteristic ease of workability which places them in a special category.

It is believed that the discovery of gold, silver and copper in a native state (i.e., the pure form found in nature) led to the first use of metal by man. The development of metallurgy – the art of separating metals from their ores, and then working them – was the result of finding ways to use gold and silver. No functional application was invented for these metals as, unlike copper, they are too soft for making implements, early man's prime interest. Their first use was therefore for decorative purposes.

At an early date man understood their outstanding qualities of *ductility* (ability to be

150 *Right* A pair of large ear-pendants made from beetle-wing cases (*elytrae*). They are decorated with feathers and have human hair on their ends. Perhaps made by the Jivaro people, Ecuador.

151 *Below* Necklace of the Kikuyu, Kenya, made of snake vertebrae threaded on a leather thong.

152 A married woman's head-dress of gold, decorated with beaded wire and studded with turquoise and brown stone beads. This piece is thought to be of Mongolian origin, but similar items are made over a wide area of Central Asia by Chinese craftsmen to local specifications.

formed into wire); *malleability* (ability to be formed into sheet); *fusibility* (ability to be melted to make a casting); *lustre* (ability to be polished and to acquire an attractive finish); and *durability*, all of which made these metals eminently suited to be worked by the many decorative processes eventually invented in jewellery-making. Many of these same techniques were also applied to other metals and alloys.

Thus each material developed its own technology according to its basic nature. In some cases the technology employed is unique to a particular material; in others the experience already learned for one material was transferred to another that could be worked with the same tools. In such cases technology advanced that much more rapidly.

Local resources were always of prime importance, but many exotic materials, even in early times, came to a people by elaborate foreign and intertribal trade networks. The economics of trade, for instance, explain why in India huge quantities of gold, which became available when traders from Europe paid in gold for local raw materials and spices, were used for ornaments. Another example involving non-metallic materials occurred in land-locked Tibet, far from any marine resources. Overland trade brought the Tibetans red coral from the Mediterranean; amber from the Baltic; and pearls and mother-of-pearl from tropical waters. All these were – and continue to be – highly valued because of their exotic nature, and they are widely employed in Tibetan jewellery. Once non-local materials such as these were available on a regular basis, the jeweller's ingenuity was challenged to invent new designs and technologies to employ them. The knowledge and approach to design which developed was passed from one generation to another, ultimately to become the traditional culture of that society, based upon exotica.

Not uncommonly, commercial contact also introduced non-indigenous technologies. An example is the glass-bead work and silver jewellery of the American Indians. Seed beads from Venice and Bohemia came to them only after first contacts with European foreigners, who used beads as a medium of establishing friendships, and for barter. Along with these materials came the basic technology of their use: stringing, appliqué beadwork and loom weaving with beads. Some of this technology was related to existing quillwork, but beads, because of their regularity in size, required far more varied systems of work, especially in terms of design. The latter often incorporated purely indigenous motifs that gave the objects they created a unique appearance. Ultimately, despite the original foreign source of these materials and techniques, beadwork came to be associated with American Indian culture, and is now thought of as being 'typically' American Indian.

Another important means of technological diffusion was the migration or invasion of peoples, who brought the knowledge of their technological achievements with them. In some cases their degree of technological development was superior to the people they contacted or conquered, and in others, that of the people they dominated was superior. Often an amalgamation of the two took place to produce an innovative technology.

Jewellers' tools

The production of ornaments of metal, or other materials, requires a range of tools and techniques, some specifically suited to a particular function or material. Each tool embodies the collective experience of countless generations. Increasing expertise and mastery over particular techniques led in some cases to specialisation, which in turn resulted in the need for co-operation between the various craftsmen who may have worked in sequence upon the same object at various stages in its manufacture.

The average ethnic jeweller still uses tools of the most ancient and primitive forms. He probably does not employ more than about forty tools, but with these he carries out all

153 Two goldsmiths shown at work in a Company School drawing, c. 1850. Spread on the floor before them are various tools used in jewellery-making: tongs, a drawplate, hammers, a blowing tube, a crucible, an ingot mould, pincers and a fire-fan. The goldsmith on the left is hammering a rod of precious metal on an anvil to make an anklet; a finished anklet lies on the floor beside him. The other is blowing through a bamboo tube to increase the fire temperature while soldering an ornament, which he handles with tongs. At his feet is another anvil. The tools shown are identical with those used by goldsmiths in India today.

the processes needed to complete the often complex jewellery he makes. In some cases an entire 'workshop' is portable, and can be carried in one leather handbag. In the past this was often a necessity when a jeweller worked for nomadic people, who moved seasonally with their animals to better grazing grounds.

Tools used for metalwork, and also work on other materials, can be divided into categories according to the basic manner of their use:

Holding tools are designed to grasp an object in order to free partially or completely a jeweller's hand or hands for other work. They include vices of various kinds, clamps to hold parts temporarily together, tweezers, pliers and tongs to hold cold or hot work in progress.

Striking or percussion tools are among the oldest invented. Their function is to transform the basic metal into the desired form. These include all sorts of mallets and hammers which are made in many weights, sizes and shapes, serving specific functions. Hammers are also used for indirect striking, to activate other tools such as die-punches, repoussé and chasing punches, chisels or rivet setters.

Compression tools are of two types: passive and active. Passive compression tools include anvils, stakes, mandrels, and dapping dies – all used as a surface to counteract the impact of other tools upon the metal object placed over them during work. Active compression tools are those used directly upon the object, and include the rolling mill, the burnisher used to finish a metal surface, and tools employed in stone-setting, such as bezel setters, beaders and prong setters.

Cutting tools have sharp edges or teeth, both meant to sever or shear metal. The most important of the severing tools is the jeweller's saw, which cuts metal by attrition. Shearing tools which cut by the opposition of two cutting blades include various forms of metal hand shears. Impact shearing is done with a sharp-edged contour-cutting die which is struck with a hammer to cut a shape out of sheet metal when the intention is to make several duplicates.

Metal-removal tools work on the principle of attrition or metal removal by a rubbing, reciprocal or shaving action. These include boring tools which work by rotational shaving action, such as the hand-drill, strap-drill or pump-drill – all very ancient – and awls and reamers used to make or enlarge a hole. Others that work by reciprocal abrasion are files and hand scrapers.

Torsion tools are those used to set or remove a screw which must be driven in spirally. In use since Roman times, this group includes the screw driver and wrenches.

Forms of metal

The metal used by a jeweller comes in a variety of forms, which to a great extent determine the ultimate appearance of the object, and also influence which of the many decorative processes can be carried out upon it.

Bulk metal is primarily used for casting, in which hot viscous metal is poured into a mould. Rods and ingots are forms of bulk metal also used for casting purposes, but can themselves be processed further, for example by forging, as when making a torc, and the result can be decorated by chip-carving and pattern stamping.

Sheet metal allows a range of processes such as cutting, sawing, cold bending, doming, piercing, die-stamping, raising and filing. The surface decoration possible on sheet metal includes repoussé and chasing, stamped work, engraving and inlay work.

Tubing can be used for both functional purposes, such as making hinges, and decorative processes. In ethnic jewellery tubing is generally made from sheet metal and therefore has a longitudinal seam which, when necessary, must be soldered closed.

154 Silver anklet from Rajasthan, India. The upper part is a sheet metal tube (the horizontal seam is visible on the inside), joined to the lower sheet-metal part. The tube is ornamented with wrapped wire and petal-shapes made from stamped shot; the lower part has applied stamped squares and divisions of pattern-stamped ornamental wire. On the front are four large shots, the upper one backed by a stylised sun-disc.

Wire is used for both structural and decorative purposes. Heavy- or lightweight wire can be cold-forged to taper or change its sectional form. Wire is commonly used for making chain, often an important element in ethnic jewellery, and has many decorative uses, including pattern-stamping and filigree work. It can be twisted to form various types of spiral; wrapped, plaited or interwoven.

Basic metal jewellery techniques

We have seen that a great many non-metallic materials have been, and are still used in ethnic jewellery manufacture. In the minds of most people, however, jewellery means *metal* jewellery, and usually the precious metals gold and silver are implied. Metalworking techniques are divided into those that require the use of heat, and those that do not. Cold construction methods include cold-forging, riveting, screwing, flanging, and the use of the lathe. Hot construction methods are hot-forging, fusing and casting. These techniques cannot all be discussed here, but for the sake of illustration the most important in each of these groups can be briefly described: cold-forging and hot-casting.

Cold-forging

Forging can be carried out by hot or cold methods. Gold and silver can be cold-forged because these metals can take a considerable amount of compression before they become work-hardened. At that time, if work is to be continued, they need to be softened, and this is done by a heating process called *annealing*, repeated each time the object becomes again work-hardened.

Forging metal, which is usually in the form of a rod or heavy wire, includes stretching, shrinking, tapering or bending it. The metal is hammered while being held upon a resisting surface such as an anvil. When struck, the metal moves in a direction determined by the angle of the hammer blow. The form of the hammer face – flat, convex or narrow – also affects the change that takes place in the metal being worked.

155   The basic forging processes are *rounding* (to change the cross-section from square to round); *drawing down* (gradually to increase the metal in length without increasing it in width); *setting down* (to reduce the area worked in section); *spreading* (to increase the width, either at its end or at an intermediate position); and *upsetting* (to thicken the metal edgewise by hammering).

Metal rods can also be bent, slit and cut out by the use of hammers and cold chisels. A twist can be imparted to a square or rectangular sectioned rod by first annealing the metal, then rotating one end, which is grasped with pliers, while the other end is immobilised. Other characteristic techniques of forging are forming a spiral; punching a hole with a pointed instrument which is driven through the metal; collaring two parts together by the use of an encircling ring or band; and wrapping a heavier rod with lighter-weight wire.

Forging, like all other metalworking processes, creates a distinctive appearance which is easily recognisable, and can be noted in such jewellery as torcs made in India and Afghanistan, and in some of the jewellery of Morocco.

155 A silver torc from Gujarat, India, forged from a single rod of metal and ornamented with wrapped wire. The circlet closure is decorated with pattern-stamped flat discs.

CASTING

The essential prerequisite for the development of metallurgy was that metal could be melted if heated to a high enough temperature, after which it could be given a controllable new form by casting. Moulds are required to contain the liquefied metal until it has cooled and solidified. Moulds have been made of a variety of materials, each capable of withstanding the necessarily high temperatures needed to melt the different metals used by jewellers. They include stone, such as steatite or talc, which is conveniently soft enough to be carved easily to form a negative of the object inside the mould; cuttlebone, the internal skeleton of the cuttlefish; refractory clays; and later also iron or steel.

Moulds can be constructed in one piece, in both open and closed types, or in two or more pieces. The choice of mould type used often depends on whether only a single, unique object is to be cast, or if several repeats are to be made of the object, using the same mould. Various cultures seem to have shown a preference for different mould types, the choice depending on the kind of objects they made.

When an open, one-piece mould is used, the result is a solid object with a three-dimensional face and a flat back. This type of mould is often reusable for making repeats of the same casting, until the cavity surface that contacts the molten metal loses its accuracy after repeated use and disintegrates. A closed one-piece mould usually results in a three-dimensional form in-the-round. In the process of freeing the object, after the metal has solidified and cooled sufficiently for the casting to be extracted, the mould is destroyed, so it can be used only once. Two-piece moulds usually have the negative half of the object in each part, and the two mould parts are keyed to fit accurately together. Two-part moulds without undercuts are often reusable, and they are made of stone, metal or, less usually, of clay.

Gravity pour casting is the simplest and most ancient casting system. In this method the molten metal is poured into an open or closed mould and its sheer weight, aided by the pull of gravity, causes it to fill the mould void.

Lost-wax casting is a method that requires the construction of a full-sized model in wax. Herein lies the artistry of the technique, as once the wax model is completed the remaining processes of casting are completely mechanical. In some cases the model is made of solid wax, which means that its entire volume will be replaced by metal in the resulting casting. With gold, because of the metal's high value, the model is made as thin as the technique will allow; if the spaces in the mould are too narrow, the metal cools and solidifies before it can completely fill the mould void. When this happens all the work of preparing the wax model is lost, the unsuccessful, incomplete casting must be discarded, and the metal reused for another casting. Incomplete castings have been found in the area of Precolumbian Panama and Colombia, where lost-wax casting in gold was a commonly employed jewellery-making method.

When a larger object is created, to lighten its weight and economise on the amount of gold used the wax model is built up on a clay core. This approximates the form of the object, but is slightly smaller all round to allow for the thickness of the wax that will be placed upon it to create the model. To keep this core in position during the casting process, small metal rods are fixed perpendicularly through the finished wax model and penetrate the core. At the time of pouring the metal these pins hold the core suspended within the mould void. Once the casting is removed from the mould, visible pin ends are clipped away flush with the object's surface. These places can be detected if the result is carefully examined.

The finished wax model is first coated with a fine-textured clay, which assures greatest accuracy in reproducing its detail and surface texture when cast. Once this has dried,

156 *Opposite* Gold pectoral disc of the Asante, Ghana, made by professional smiths who excelled in lost-wax casting. It is of the striking type worn by kings and senior chiefs. The intricate openwork design was created by wax threads.

several additional applications of a coarser clay are made, the latter often mixed with an organic material to increase the mould porosity to permit the escape of gases generated by heat. Mould porosity occurs when the organic substance burns away during casting, leaving the mould permeated with small openings. After several clay applications have brought the mould wall to a thickness sufficiently strong to endure the heat and internal pressure, the mould is set aside to dry thoroughly.

The dry mould is placed over a prepared, bedded fire, and as it heats up any remaining moisture it contains evaporates. At a certain temperature the wax model melts out through an opening left at one end of the mould. This leaves the void within the mould that will be filled with the metal; it is this that gives the lost-wax process its name.

Metal and mould are brought separately up to the high temperature needed for the particular metal used. The crucible in which the metal has been melted is lifted with tongs, and the molten metal is poured through the opening to fill the mould. Cooling is often hastened by splashing the mould with water. When cooled, the clay mould is broken off the casting, which is cleaned. If the core is now accessible, it is removed, but if not, it remains within the object. The sprue and runner opening through which the metal passed to the mould cavity, now a funnel-shaped solid attached to the casting, are cut away. The object is finished and polished.

The lost-wax casting process has been used all over the world. It reached a high state of refinement and control in the cast gold jewellery of the Asante in Ghana, and the Sinú of Columbia, whose jewellery characteristically consisted of elaborate compositions made with very thin wax rods, as in nose ornaments which look almost like filigree work. Casting objects of such delicacy is difficult, therefore the achievement is evidence of laudatory skill. In some cultures more than one metalworking technique may be used to produce an object, including casting; for example, Türkmen sheet-metal cuff bracelets, whose openings are lined with a series of dentated projecting cast prongs. Small castings may be used to ornament the surface of objects made by other techniques.

Decorative techniques

None of the basic metalworking techniques the jeweller uses knows ethnic or geographic boundaries. Jewellers everywhere have practised them from early times. Embellishment constitutes another, secondary area of exploration and experiment. The pleasure in the ornamentation may be partly for the decoration itself, but the satisfaction of the maker in his own skill is likely to be important too.

The elaboration of jewellery by surface decoration generally involves no structural alteration of its basic form and takes place subsequent to its creation. Specialisation has sometimes come to characterise the jewellery of a particular culture, and to be associated with it. An example is the granulation work of the Etruscans (seventh to sixth centuries BC), who brought this technique to an unsurpassed peak of refinement. In truth, however, every technique at one time or another has been carried out at more than one place. As far as granulation is concerned, Western literature on jewellery has for the most part ignored its skilful execution by past and present jewellers in the East, particularly India, China, and several cultures of the Indonesian Archipelago, such as Bali, and among the Toba of Sumatra.

The decorative processes described briefly below are carried out after the object has been made, as the last stages in its production. Their execution is accomplished with a few, simple tools. It has never been customary for a jeweller to possess or use a great many tools, and all are designed specifically for the functions demanded by the particular technique. The decorative and finishing techniques used on metal jewellery can also be divided into cold- and hot-working methods.

TECHNIQUES: *bending, doming, repoussé and chasing*

Cold-work metal decorative techniques

BENDING SHEET METAL

Bending metal can be done in two ways, with or without deformation of the original flat sheet. Metal can be bent without deformation into simple angles or curves, or combinations of these, from a flat sheet in one plane into a three-dimensional form, which it retains without spring-back. In terms of decoration this type of bending includes curling, spiralling, twisting, and wrapping. Flat sheets can also be bent to enclose a volume with flat sides, such as a cube, rectangle or prism, or one with curved sides such as a cylinder or cone. In these forms the original sheet metal edges are no longer visible.

Sheet metal can be bent with deformation by the stretching or contraction of the metal. To do this the metal is generally worked with hammers and moulds. The decorative processes in this group include doming, repoussé and chasing, and die stamping – all commonly used in jewellery-making.

DOMING

157 Doming is the process of forming a hollow metal hemisphere of any diameter. A dome can either be made from a metal disc, or formed upon any part of a larger metal sheet of which it becomes an integral part. An ancient process, doming employs a *doming* or *dapping block* or *die*: a brass cube each of whose six sides has several semi-circular

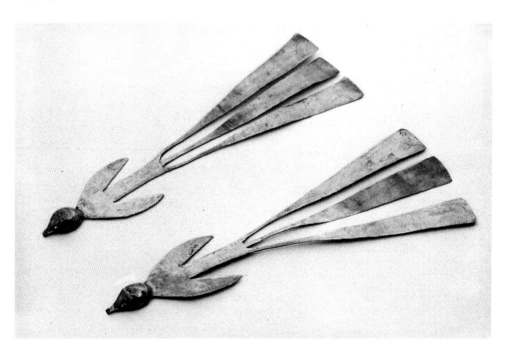

157 A pair of Precolumbian gold ear ornaments from Antioquia, Colombia. They are cut from sheet metal in the form of birds, the heads raised in relief, with the eyes defined by repoussé work.

depressions of different dimensions. The diameter of each depression matches that of a ball-ended *doming punch*. The metal is placed over the selected depression in the dapping block, and the punch placed over the metal. The end of the punch is then hammered, forcing the metal into the depression. Two domes of the same diameter soldered together make a hollow bead, and this is a common process for metal bead making. Jewellery can be ornamented with convex or concave domes using this technique.

REPOUSSÉ AND CHASING

Repoussé work takes advantage of the malleability and plasticity of sheet metal which permits it to be formed into a relief pattern. It is a deformation process: the metal is

158 A silver pendant amulet box from Patna, India. The design of opposed peacocks was created by repoussé work and chasing, with engraved details; the pendant is further embellished with small pattern stampings and pendant bells. Strung on black cord with silver melon-shaped beads.

stretched and compressed while being worked with punches from the back, causing it to bulge outwards in convex forms. In actual practice repoussé work is accompanied alternately by chasing, which is a related process also done with punches. These are generally of a finer, smaller type, intended to create detail in the design from the front, refining the forms created by repoussé.

In both repoussé and chasing the working faces of the punches used have a variety of shapes and widths. The choice of tool depends on the requirement of the design. In action a tool is placed on the metal angled *away* from the worker, and its end struck with a hammer to make it move *towards* the worker. This system permits the result to be visible while the work is in progress.

159 Two die-stamped ornaments from Rajasthan, India, both showing Hanuman, the monkey deity. The pendant (*phul deota*) was worn on a necklace cord, and the three-part ornament was worn on the upper arm bound by a cord.

During work the object is held by a compound of pitch combined with a stiffening substance such as brick dust or plaster of paris. This is either spread on a board, or contained in a heavy, cast-iron round-bottomed bowl that rests on a loose ring so it can be tilted in any direction. This black, tar-like material has enough resilience to give way under the force of the blows, and tenacity to hold the object in place. When work-hardening occurs, the object is removed from the pitch compound, cleaned, annealed to soften it, and possibly replaced in a reversed position.

Hollow jewellery, such as the wrist and ankle bracelets of India, Iran, Oman and elsewhere, may be decorated by filling the hollow with pitch, then working the design with chasing tools only from the outer surface. Once the work is finished, the object is heated to make the pitch flow out.

STAMPING

Stamping is an old method developed to save time and effort should a design call for many repeats of identical units. There are three basic stamping techniques: blanking, embossing and impressing.

155 *Blanking* results in a flat shape (a blank), which is cut out of a sheet of metal with a blanking punch alone or with a combination of punch and die. This can either be used as it stands in the form of, say, a flat disc, or processed further so that the disc can, for instance, simulate a coin.

160 Brass hand-stamping dies from Kantillo, Orissa, India. The patterns are typical of those used in contemporary jewellery. From the large round die a single unit is selected for making a small die-stamped element, a type commonly used to cover a join.

Embossing involves placing the metal over an open stamping die which contains an intaglio pattern. A piece of sheet metal is placed over it and hammered, forcing it into the die. It then takes its form as a positive in relief. Examples of this technique are the silver amulets commonly worn in India on which Hindu deities are depicted.

Impressing is the direct stamping of a punch bearing a design on its face onto a finished object. The work is held upon a resisting surface; the punch is held in position where the design is wanted, and the punch is struck with a hammer, usually with a single blow to get a clear design impression. Innumerable design punches are used in jewellery, their designs usually having some broader symbolic significance within the particular culture that uses them.

PIERCING

Metal may be pierced for either functional or decorative purposes. Piercing can be carried out with various tools. In the Middle East and India piercing is often done from the front of a hollow object, such as a bracelet, using small sharp cold chisels. The resulting sharp cut edges of the pierced opening turn inwards towards the hollow, out of harm's way. The same technique was carried out on ancient Roman pierced-work jewellery and was called *opus interrasile* ('opening work'). A more modern method of pierced-work is done with a jeweller's saw. A small hole is drilled through the metal and a saw blade threaded through; the area to be removed is then sawn out.

Holes can also be made in an object by drilling through the metal; boring through it with a pointed awl or reamer; or hammering a pointed tool through the metal.

CHIP-CARVING

40 Chip-carving was a method widely practised in Scandinavia during Viking times, and is used elsewhere today. Small sharp chisels are used to carve a pattern in a relatively thick metal object, the pattern appearing in relief.

METAL INLAY

62 Metal inlay involves the insertion of one metal into a groove or depression made in a second metal of a contrasting colour. Because the groove in the host metal has an undercut, the inlaid metal is permanently fixed in place, mechanically held in the groove by the acute angle of the undercut. An inlay can be linear, made with wire, or a unit of sheet metal of any shape. It is placed in the groove or excavated area and a hammer is used to force the undercut edge over the inlaid metal which fixes it in place.

Several variations on the technique are possible. Usually the inlay is flush with the surface of the host metal, but it can also be left in relief. A sheet metal inlay can have been previously ornamented with a stamped, carved, engraved or repoussé pattern. If it is in high relief, it is usual for the depressions on its reverse side to be filled with a substance such as lac to support the relief and make the back level. Relief inlays are often referred to as encrustations. The inlay may be further ornamented after being applied to the object by stamping, engraving, or the use of other techniques.

ENGRAVING

Engraving is the highly skilled art of making decorative incisions into the surface of metal with the aid of various sharp-pointed engravers or burins, either on flat or completely

161 Engraved silver bracelets of the Haida, North-west Coast of America. The making of silver bracelets engraved with conventionalised animal forms began on the North-west Coast during the 19th century. Innovations by modern artists include shaping the bracelet in the form of the animal depicted. These examples were collected in the 1980s.

three-dimensional objects. The shape and angle of the tool's cutting edge determines the character of the groove. Engraving metal (it is also possible to engrave other materials such as ivory) removes thin slivers from the parent metal. The hand-held burin is worked in a direction *away* from the worker – unlike chasing, with which this technique is unwarily compared. (In chasing *no* metal is removed from the object.) Linear or textural effects can be made, and entire surfaces can be covered with engraved designs, as in the ₁₆₁ case of the jewellery of the Haida Indians of Alaska, and the Tuareg of Morocco and Mauritania.

The engraved grooves are initially bright, but oxidise in time, leaving the design as black lines on a light ground (the surface of the object).

THE DECORATIVE USES OF WIRE

Wire, one of the basic forms of metal, has many uses in the decoration of jewellery. Different effects are possible, depending on the cross-section and dimension of the wire. Round wire is most common, but square wire and flat strip are also widely used. Compound fabrics made of two or more round wires can be twisted together for cable-like effects, and this form is commonly used for borders, as well as for filigree construction. Square-sectioned wire can be given a self-twist, the edges forming ridged spirals. Round wire and flat wire strip lend themselves to wrapping, a common form of jewellery decoration, and also to plaiting, braiding and other interwoven techniques.

The cross-section of wire can be altered by drawing it with drawtongs through a drawplate with openings of various shapes. Wire can be stamped with a repeat pattern, for instance to give it the appearance of a series of small beads. This is called beaded wire, and is commonly used for borders in the jewellery of Nepal and Tibet. Wire stamped with geometric or floral patterns is commonly used in India to make the half-round bangles worn everywhere.

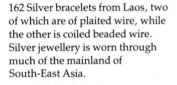

162 Silver bracelets from Laos, two of which are of plaited wire, while the other is coiled beaded wire. Silver jewellery is worn through much of the mainland of South-East Asia.

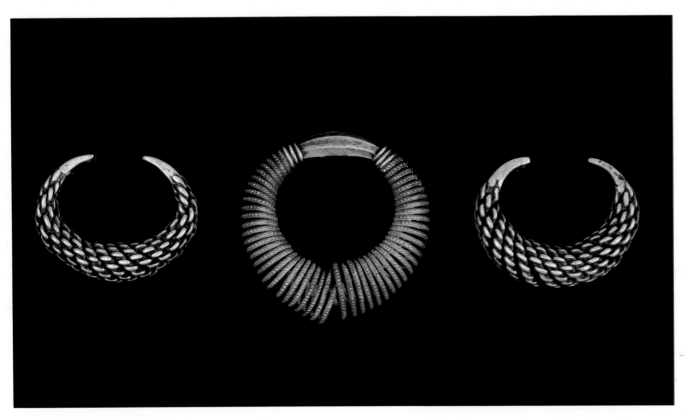

163 Precolumbian pendant from Popayan, Colombia, cast by the lost-wax method in *tumbaga*, a gold-copper alloy. The surface has been enriched by the technique of depletion gilding.

A piece of jewellery can be decorated with applied wire of various forms, or it can be made entirely of wire, as in filigree work. A common use of spirally twisted wire can be seen, for example, in the bracelets worn by the Lao, in South-East Asia.

GOLD LEAF

Gold leaf is usually a pure (24 carat) or almost pure gold. Among ethnic peoples gold leaf is usually laboriously hammered by hand into very thin sheets. Gold is especially suited to this process, as it is very malleable and ductile. Silver is also made into leaf, but in ethnic jewellery the use of gold leaf is more common.

Gold leaf can be mechanically applied cold to a metal base or a non-metallic material, such as wood. An example of the latter is the huge gold-leaf covered wooden bracelets worn by some chiefs in Ghana. The gold leaf is applied to the base which has been prepared with a coating of resin or glue to which it readily adheres. Its function is to make the object appear to be made entirely of gold.

DEPLETION GILDING

Depletion gilding is a cold-finishing method used with objects made of a gold alloy of any composition. To create a surface appearance of the characteristic bright yellow colour of pure gold the surface must be freed of any alloying metal which changes its colour. To do this the object is first heated to oxidise the non-gold molecules on the surface. It is then immersed in a hot, dilute acid solution which dissolves the surface oxidation but does not affect the gold present. The process is repeated until all the non-gold alloying metal is removed from the surface, leaving it covered with pure gold. A more lasting finish is achieved by rubbing the surface with a burnisher, which compresses the gold molecules and hardens the gold, without removing any of it. This method was commonly used in the Precolumbian goldwork of Central and South America, and it is still practised in India and elsewhere, especially in places where mechanical polishing lathes are not in use. Another form of gilding used in jewellery that requires heat (fire gilding) is described on p. 198.

STONE-SETTING

Stone-setting must be a cold-working process, because most stones used in jewellery cannot withstand heat without being damaged or destroyed. This subject is too vast to be discussed here. It can be briefly mentioned, however, that in most ethnic jewellery the stones used are table- or cabochon-cut, and not the faceted type. Faceted stones are an indication of recent Western influence. In some cultures the tradition of using carved stones continues, as in the jewellery of China, India, Nepal and Tibet.

Most stones are set in closed bezel settings. In places like India, Nepal and Tibet stones are commonly set on a supporting bed of lac that fills most of the bezel interior. It is a common practice in these places when translucent stones are used to increase their light-reflecting brilliance and colour by placing metallic foil, sometimes coloured, below the stones. To hold the stone in place the top edge of the bezel is burnished over the stone's sloping perimeter. In some work, such as the jewellery of Kazakhstan, USSR, where red glass is used as a cornelian substitute, the stone's flat upper surface is protected and decorated at the same time by fixing a metal, geometrically patterned openwork plate over it.

Stone mosaics are commonly used in the jewellery of Nepal and Tibet. Some of these stones may be within bezels, but most are simply fixed to a ground of lac by heating the stone only sufficiently to melt the lac and form a firm bond with the stone. In these mosaics it is common to find carved stones.

Hot-work metal decorative techniques

SHOT FUSING

Fusion, or the melting of metal by heat, is a method of decorating jewellery, as well as joining parts, as in soldering, and granulation work. Heat is applied to melt either the entire piece of metal (total fusion), or its surface only (partial or surface fusion).

Total fusion occurs when making shot, a small, solid ball, commonly used as a decorative element in ethnic jewellery. To make a piece of shot, a small amount of metal, either scrap or wire, is heated until it melts completely. When this occurs the metal is naturally drawn into the form of a ball because the force of surface tension in the molten metal seeks to contract the mass into a form with the smallest possible surface area, which 154 is a sphere. Shot is used on jewellery in its usual round form as an accent that catches highlights. It may also be hammered flat into a disc and soldered into place, often to cover a join, for example where two parts of border wire meet. The jewellery of the Toba in Sumatra, and the Kabyle people of the Atlas Mountain area in North Africa (Algeria and Morocco) commonly employs shot, large and small.

GRANULATION

Granulation utilises both forms of fusion: total fusion to create small granules, and surface fusion to form the welding bond that joins the granules to the surface of the object 164 they decorate. In this ancient process work begins with the making of the tiny granules. This is done by using small snippets of wire, or coarse filings of gold or silver, sprinkled in several layers on pulverised charcoal placed in a metal container. The box with its metal contents is heated till the scraps melt and contract automatically into miniature balls, as described above. The charcoal is washed away, leaving the metal balls at the bottom of the container. As the design usually calls for granules of several sizes, the balls are sorted into several uniform diameters by passing them through a series of meshes, the smallest first, followed by increasingly larger sizes.

The granules are placed upon the object's surface with tweezers, or a wet brush with which they are lifted one at a time. As this is done each ball is coated with the fluxing liquid on the brush. (If tweezers are used, the ball is first dipped into this solution.) The liquid contains an organic glue and some form of copper, such as a copper salt, or a copper solid, such as an oxide ground into very fine particle size. The glue holds the small granule in position, but also serves another purpose. When it is heated, the glue carbonises and interacts chemically with the copper present, causing the surface of both granule and object to melt at a lower temperature than the rest of the metal. At this time the copper runs to the point of contact between the granule and base and there forms a small metal fillet consisting of an alloying of the copper and the gold (or silver) on the molten surface of the granule and object. This bonds the granule in place at the tiny point of contact with the base. The join is almost invisible, and this is the basis of the appeal of the granulation process.

Making the bonding join between granule and base requires critical judgement as to the exact moment when the jeweller's torch flame must be withdrawn. Should heating be prolonged longer than necessary, the overheated object can collapse. Granulation is still practised in India, Bali, Sumatra, and elsewhere.

NIELLO

Niello is another decorative process that requires the heat of fusion. Its black colour, from which it derives its (Italian) name, takes advantage of the colour contrast between itself 28 and the parent metal of the object, usually gold or silver, into which it is inlaid.

The niello technique is widespread. Formerly it was practised in Central Asian

164 *Opposite* Detail of a Chinese hairpin of the Tang dynasty (7th-8th century). The pin consists of U-shaped silver-gilt prongs. On the upper part of the pin the space between the prongs is richly ornamented with wirework scrolls and flowers, and embellished with granulation. The lower part has a sheet-gold motif of a bird set against a granulated background. The empty setting originally contained semi-precious stones.

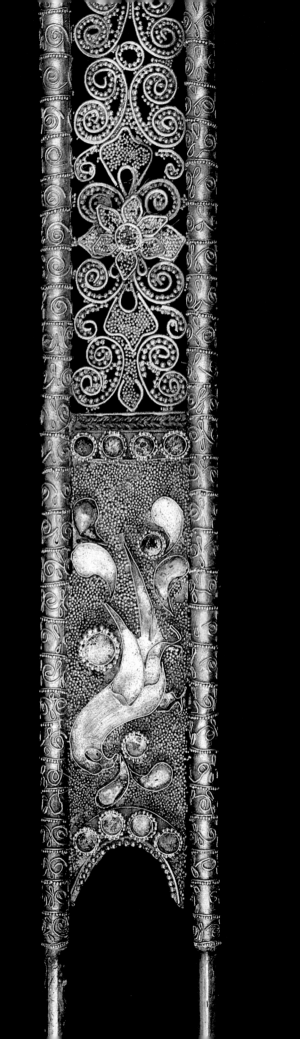

Turkestan, the Russian Caucasus region, and Turkey. Presently it is carried out, among other places, in Tula and Veliky Ustiug in the USSR, southern Morocco, and in Bangkok, Thailand.

Niello is a tri-metal alloy of silver, copper and lead, each in specific proportions. These are fused together by heat and the addition of sulphur, which causes the result ultimately to become black, also forming them into a metallic sulphide compound – niello. While viscous the compound is poured onto a metal surface and allowed to cool and solidify. As the compound is brittle, it can be pulverised with mortar and pestle into a fine, black powder.

It is applied to the parent metal in a similar manner to champlevé enamelling. The powder is mixed into a paste by the addition of a borax or sal ammoniac flux which aids it to flow when heated. This is loaded with a spatula into the previously prepared design depressions made in the object by chasing or engraving tools. After drying by the application of heat, the niello compound is fused and fills the depressions, becoming durably and permanently bonded to the base metal. Any surplus niello is removed from the surface either by scraping it away with a sharp knife, or by the use of an abrasive stick, which brings the niello level with the parent metal. After the surface is polished the formerly negative design depression, now niello filled, appears as a black pattern, with either the niello as the ground of the figure, or as the design figure itself.

ENAMELLING

Enamel is a glass-like substance whose composition, and rate of expansion and contraction when fused and cooled, is compatible with that of the metals upon which it is placed, mainly copper, silver and gold. The use of enamel to ornament jewellery goes back to ancient Egyptian, Greek and Byzantine times. Later on the art of enamelling was practised at various European, North African, Iranian, Indian and Chinese centres. The history of its development and diffusion is complicated and fascinating, but cannot be gone into here.

There are several basic enamelling techniques used in jewellery-making, each with its special appearance. In each technique design treatment varies from place to place. The enamelling techniques used by ethnic jewellers are champlevé, cloisonné and, to a lesser extent, painted enamel. Other enamelling techniques are not discussed here as they are not used in ethnic jewellery.

In champlevé enamelling grooves are excavated in the base metal with small chisels, chasing tools or gravers. As in the case of niello, the grooves are then filled with powdered enamel to which water and gum are added to make a paste. Once dry, the object is fired, either over a heat source such as a bed of charcoal, or in a kiln. At the point of enamel fusion the object is removed from the heat source in a red-hot state and set aside to cool. In the firing process the original paste volume of the enamel shrinks due to the heat, and it is usually necessary to refill the depressions with additional enamel of the same colour and fire the object again. The process can be repeated until the enamel fills the depressions, or left at a point when they are less than filled and the enamel surface is concave. If the aim is to produce a smooth, level surface, the enamel is ground to a level with the parent metal, then polished or given a final firing to restore its glassy surface lustre.

In cloisonné enamelling rectangular-sectioned or double-strand twisted wire is used to create miniature, upright walls or *cloisons* that act to separate each of the colours used. In some places where this technique is practised these walls are first soldered to the object; elsewhere the *cloisons* are glued to a pre-fired, enamel-covered surface, then filled with the coloured enamels required in the design. Several applications of enamel are again

165 One of a pair of silver armlets worn by Kabyle women on important occasions. The coral inlays and blue, yellow and green cloisonné enamel decoration are typical of the Kabyle smiths working in north Algeria.

usually needed to bring the enamel to the height of the *cloisons*, each requiring a sequence of application, drying and firing. As in champlevé enamelling, the enamel may be left at a different height from the *cloison*; this may be seen in the enamelled silver jewellery of the Kabyle (Algeria). Otherwise, the entire surface is ground down to the level of the *cloison* wires, then either refired to restore surface gloss, or polished, sometimes on a lathe.

A form of painted enamel is practised on jewellery in Benares, India, where it is called Benares 'pink enamel' (see p. 89). This technique is European in origin, and was practised in Qajar Persia.

FILIGREE

Filigree work also requires heat in its execution. A piece of jewellery in filigree consists of wire of various thicknesses and sectional shapes. Normally, the entire object is constructed in backless openwork, but the wirework may be joined to a sheet-metal backing.

Filigree work has an ancient past, and old Greek, Roman, Byzantine and Islamic examples are extant. In more recent times the technique has been carried out in places as far apart as Iceland, Portugal, Greece, Hungary, Russia, Algeria, Israel, Jordan, Tunisia,

166 Pair of silver filigree bracelets from Madras, India, in openwork filigree, with a sheet-metal backed filigree clasp. These cuffs well illustrate the original meaning of the word filigree (*filum* = wire; *granum* = grain or bead), by its typical use of these forms of metal.

Yemen, India, and is still practised today. The work is labour-intensive, which probably explains why it is carried out in places where labour costs are relatively low. The technique uses a minimum of material, which, combined with low labour cost, keeps the prices of objects low.

In filigree work wires of at least two weights are used. A heavier square- or rectangular-sectioned wire is needed for structural strength and is used to outline the main forms and major divisions in the design. A lighter-weight pattern wire, often made of two fine-gauge round wires twisted together and flattened, is used to fill in design details within the outer, heavier frame wires. In most places the forms of filler wire are standardised, and they are designed to permit the outer frame to be compactly filled.

To hold the parts together, in normal practice, the assembled work is placed on a sheet of mica, and a mixture of gum, flux (borax) and fine particles of solder is painted on the main junctions. In another method, without gum, dry flux and solder are dusted over the work. It is heated to the melting point of the solder, which flows between points of wire contact, and holds the parts together.

MERCURY AMALGAM FIRE-GILDING

This is a hot-finishing method used to make any of the non-gold metals used for jewellery look like gold. This is done by plating the object with an alloy of mercury and gold, called an amalgam. The technique was carried out in Europe from Roman and Viking times, and in the Far East in China, India and other places.

Mercury has the property of easily combining with gold and silver (as well as other metals) at room temperature (at which it is liquid), without the use of heat, to form the amalgam. To accomplish this, finely divided particles or foil of the second metal (gold or silver in the case of jewellery) are brought together with the mercury and form the paste-like substance of the amalgam. This is applied to cover part or all of the cleaned surface of the metal object. Because of its nature, the amalgam readily 'wets' and adheres to the surface.

Fire-gilding is so called because the process of eliminating the mercury and leaving the gold behind requires heat. The object is heated to a temperature somewhat above the boiling point of mercury (675°F; 356.9°C), which causes the mercury to volatilise in the form of visible fumes. When these rising mercury vapours cease to be visible the mercury is eliminated, and the object remains coated with a layer of the other metal (gold or silver). This appears dull, and must be polished to brightness by hand-burnishing. The process may be repeated to make the precious metal coating more even, or thicker.

Mercury amalgam gilding was the main gilding method employed worldwide until electroplating superseded it in the nineteenth century. It results in a heavier plating than electroplating, and is therefore longer-lasting. This has been proved by finds of ancient fire-gilded objects in which the gilding has actually acted to prevent disintegration of the object, because gold is inert and hardly reacts at all, when in a pure state, with surrounding elements.

Ethnic jewellery on which the fire-gilding method was commonly used includes the
144 silver jewellery of the Türkmen tribes of the Transcaspian region, and the Uzbeks and
35 Kazaks.

By comparison with the techniques described here, those now available in the modern industrialised world have added considerably to the precision and exactitude of the jeweller's art. Particular results and effects can be more readily controlled and reliably produced. In the end, however, recognition of the increased range and efficiency of such sophisticated technologies only heightens the sense of the levels of skill and achievement evident in the field of ethnic jewellery.

Further reading

ABEL-VIDOR, S. *et al. Between Continents/Between Seas: Precolumbian Art of Costa Rica.* New York, 1981.

ADAIR, J. *The Navajo and Pueblo Silversmiths.* Oklahoma, 1945.

ALEXANDER, C. *Jewelry: Art of the Goldsmith in Classical Times.* New York, 1928.

AL-JADIR, S. *Arab and Islamic Silver.* London, 1981.

ALKAZI, R. *Ancient Indian Costume.* New Delhi, 1983.

ARKELL. A. J. 'Cambay and the Bead Trade', *Antiquity* x, no. 39, September 1936.

ARTS COUNCIL OF GREAT BRITAIN. *Sacred Circles* (exhibition catalogue). London, 1976.

ATIL, E. *The Age of Sultan Suleyman the Magnificent.* Washington, 1987.

AZIZ, A. *The Imperial Treasury of the Indian Mughuls.* Lahore, 1942.

BARROW, T. *The Art of Tahiti.* London, 1979.

BHATTACHARYYA, B. *Gem Therapy.* Calcutta, 1976 (rev. edn).

BHUSHAN, J. B. *Indian Jewellery, Ornaments and Decorative Designs.* Bombay, 1964.

BIEBUCK, D. P. AND VAN DE ABBEELE. *The Power of Head-dresses.* Brussels, 1984.

BOWEN, R. L. 'The Olu of Itsekiris' in *Nigeria Magazine*, no. 22, 1944.

BRAIN, R. *The Decorated Body.* London, 1979.

BRITTAIN, A., WOLPERT, S. AND MORTON, P. *Engraving on Precious Metals.* London, 1973.

BROTTEM, B. V. AND LANG, A. 'Zulu Beadwork' in *African Arts*, vol. 6, 1973.

BROWNE, ST J. O. 'An African Shell ornament known as "kibangwa"', *Journal of African Studies*, vol. 29, 1930.

BRUNEL, F. *Jewellery of India.* New Delhi, 1972.

CAREY, M. *Beads and beadwork of East and South Africa.* London, 1986.

CARLI, E. *Pre-conquest Goldsmith's Work of Colombia.* London, 1957.

CARLYLE, T. *Sartor Resartus.* London, 1967 (originally pub. 1836).

CELLINI, B. *Abhandlungen über die Goldschmiedekunst und die Bildhauerei. (Treatises on the Arts of Goldsmithing and Sculpture)*, edited by R. and M. Fröhlich, Basel, 1979.

CLARK, J. D. 'Ilorin stone bead making', *Nigeria Magazine*, no. 77, 1963.

COLE, H. M. 'Living Art among the Samburu', *in* J. M. Cordwell and R. A. Schwarz (eds), *The Fabrics of Culture.* The Hague, 1979.

COLE, H. M. 'Artistic and communicative values of beads in Kenya and Ghana', *Bead Journal*, vol. 1, no. 3, 1975.

COOMARASWAMY, K. *The Indian Craftsman.* London, 1909.

CUZNER, B. *Goldsmiths' Handbook.* London, 1936.

DAVEY, N. K. *Netsuke.* London, 1974.

DAVIES, O. *West Africa before the Europeans,* London, 1967.

DOCKSTADER, F. J. *Indian Art in America.* Connecticut, 1961.

DONGERKERY, K. S. *Jewellery and Personal Adornment in India.* Delhi, 1971.

DOZIER, E. P. *The Kalinga of Northern Luzon, Philippines.* San Francisco, 1967.

EBIN, V. *The Body Decorated.* London, 1979.

EDWARDS, K. *Lost Wax Casting of Jewelry.* Chicago, 1975.

EWERS, J. C. *Hair Pipes in Plains Indian Adornment.* Smithsonian Institution, Bureau of American Ethnology Bulletin, 164. Washington, 1957.

FEDER, N. *American Indian Art.* New York, 1971.

FIROUZ, I. A. *Silver Ornaments of the Turkoman.* Tehran, 1978.

FISCH, A. *Textile Techniques in Metal.* New York, 1975.

FISHER, A. *Africa Adorned.* London, 1984.

FLINT INSTITUTE OF ARTS. *Art of the Great Lakes Indians* (exhibition catalogue). 1973.

FORBES, R. J. *Studies in Ancient Technology 5.* Leiden, 1966.

FRANK, L. *Indian Silver Jewellery of the Southwest 1868–1930.* Boston, 1978.

FREDERICKSON, N. J. AND GIBB, S. *The Covenant Chain.* Ottawa, 1980.

GLOVER, W. *Polynesia: The Polynesian Collection in the Ulster Museum, Belfast.* Belfast, n.d.

HAQUE, Z. *Gahana, Jewellery of Bangladesh.* Dhaka, 1984.

HAWLEY, R. *Omani Silver.* London/New York, 1978.

HECHTER-SCHULZ, K. 'Wire bangles, a record of Bantu craft, *South African Journal of Science*, vol. 29, 1930.

HENDLEY, T. H. 'Indian Jewellery', *The Journal of Indian Art* XII, nos 95–107, 1909.

HIGGINS, R. A. *Greek and Roman Jewellery.* Berkeley/Los Angeles, 1980.

HITCHCOCK, M. 'Islamic Influences on Indonesian Design', *in* A. Al-Shahi (ed,), *The Diversity of the Muslim Community.* London, 1987.

HÖPFNER, G. AND HASSE, G. *Metallschmuck aus Indien.* Berlin, 1978.

HORNIMAN MUSEUM. *Folk embroidery and jewellery of Bosnia-Hercegovina* (exhibition catalogue). London, 1975.

HUTT, J. *Understanding Far Eastern Art.* Oxford, 1987.

IDIENS, D. *Pacific Art in the Royal Scottish Museum.* Edinburgh, 1982.

JACOBSON, D. 'Women and jewelry in rural India', *Main currents in Indian Sociology* II, 1976.

JENKINS, M. AND KEENE, M. *Islamic Jewellery in the Metropolitan Museum of Art.* New York, 1983.

JENKS, A. E. *The Bontoc Igorot.* Manila, 1905.

JONES, J. *et al. The Art of Precolumbian Gold, the Jan Mitchell Collection.* New York/London, 1985.

JUDSON, W. A. 'Ostrich egg-shell beds', *Bantu*, vol. 13, no. 10, 1966.

KAGEO MURAOKA AND KICHIEMON OKAMURA. *Folk Arts and Crafts of Japan.* New York, 1973.

KOCH, R. P. *Dress Clothing of the Plains Indians.* Oklahoma, 1977.

LATIF, M. *et al. Mughal Jewels.* Brussels, 1982.

LEAKEY, M. D. AND L. S. B. *Excavations at Njoro River Cave.* 1950.

LEBEUF, J-P, 'Lebrets et greniers des Falis', *Bulletin de l'Institut François d'Afrique* 15, 1953, 1321–8.

LEWIS, E. AND P. *Peoples of the Golden Triangle*. London, 1984.

LINCOLN, L. (ed). *Southwest Indian Silver from the Doneghy Collection*. Texas, 1982.

LIU, R. K. 'Simulated materials in jewellery', *Ornament*, vol. 4, no. 4, 1980.

LOWE, J. *Japanese Crafts*. London, 1983.

MACK, J. *Madagascar, Island of the Ancestors*. London, 1986.

MARYON, H. *Metalwork and Enameling*. New York, 1971 (3rd edn).

MAXWELL-HYSLOP, K. R. *Western Asiatic Jewellery c. 3000–612 BC*. London, 1971.

MCLEOD, M. D. *The Asante*. London, 1981.

MEEN, V. D. AND TUSHINGHAM, A. D. *Crown Jewels of Iran*. Toronto, 1968.

MERIEL-BUSSY, Y. *Embossing of Metal Repoussage*. New York, 1970.

MORTON, P. *Contemporary Jewelry: A Studio Handbook*. New York, 1976 (rev. edn).

MUSÉE D'ETHNOGRAPHIE, GENEVA, AND MUSÉE NATIONAL D'HISTOIRE NATURELLE, PARIS. *L'art de la plume. Indiens du Bresil*. Geneva, 1985.

NATIONAL MUSEUM OF NATURAL HISTORY. *Brazilian Indian Feather Art*. Washington, 1980.

NEWMAN, T. R. *Contemporary Southeast Asian Arts and Crafts*. New York, 1977.

OGDEN, J. *Jewellery of the Ancient World*. London, 1982.

O'HANLON, M. 'Handsome is as Handsome does: Display and Betrayal in the Wahgi', *Oceania* 53:4, 1983, 317–33.

OLIVER, D. *Ancient Tahitian Society*. Hawaii, 1974.

ORCHARD, W. C. 'Beads and Beadwork of the American Indians', in Museum of American Indians *Contributions* XI, 1929, 13.

PACK, G. *Jewelry Making by the Lost Wax Process*. New York, 1976 (rev. edn).

PHELPS, S. *Art and Artefacts of the Pacific, Africa and the Americas*. London, 1976.

POLE, L. M. *Worlds of Man: ethnography at the Saffron Walden Museum*. Saffron Walden, 1987.

POLLARD ROWE, A. *Costumes and Featherwork of the Lords of Chimor. Textiles from Peru's North Coast*. Washington, 1984.

PRESSMAR, E. *Indische Ringe*. Frankfurt am Main, 1982.

RAMSEYER, U. *The Art and Culture of Bali*. Oxford, 1977.

RODGERS, S. *Power and Gold: Jewelry from Indonesia, Malaysia and the Philippines*. Geneva, 1985.

ROGERS, J. M. AND WARD, R. M. *Süleyman The Magnificent*. London, 1988.

ROSS, H. C. *The Art of Bedouin jewellery – a Saudi Arabian profile*, Freiburg, 1981.

SCARFE, H. *Cutting and Setting Stones*. London, 1972.

SCHELE, L. AND MILLER, M. E. *The Blood of Kings, Dynasty and Ritual in Maya Art*. Fort Worth, 1986.

SCHLETZER, D. AND R. *Old silver jewellery of the Turkoman*. Berlin, 1984.

SEEGER, A. 'The meaning of Body Ornaments', *Ethnology* 14, 1975, 211–24.

SINKANKAS, J. *Gem Cutting: A Lapidary's Manual*. New York, 1962.

SKELTON, R. (ed). *The Indian Heritage: Court Life and Arts under Mughal Rule*. London, 1982.

SMITH, E. A. *Working in Precious Metals*. 1933, reprinted London, 1978.

SPINK, M. *Islamic Jewellery*. London, 1986.

STARZECKA, D. *Hawaii*. London, 1975.

STARZECKA, D. AND CRANSTONE, B. A. L. *The Solomon Islanders*. London, 1974.

STRATHERN, A. AND M. *Self-Decoration in Mount Hagen*. London, 1971.

STRATHERN, M. 'The Self in Self-Decoration', *Oceania* 49:4, 1979, 241–57.

TAIT, H. (ed). *Seven Thousand Years of Jewellery*. London, 1986.

TEWARI, S. P. *Nupura – the anklet in Indian literature and art*. Delhi, 1982.

TURNER, T. S. 'The Social Skin', in J. Cherfas and R. Lewis (eds), *Not Work Alone*. London, 1980.

TURNER, T. S. 'Tchikrin: a central Brazilian tribe and its symbolic language of bodily adornment', in *Natural History* 78, 8. 1969.

TWALA, R. G. 'Beads as regulating the social life of the Zulu and Swazi', *African Studies*, vol. 10, 1954.

TYLECOTE, R. F. *A History of Metallurgy*. London, 1976.

UNTRACHT, O. 'The ornaments of India, Nepal and Tibet', in Museum of Contemporary Art, *The Art of Adornment* (exhibition catalogue). New York, 1963.

UNTRACHT, O. *Enameling on Metal*. Pennsylvania, 1957.

UNTRACHT, O. *Jewelry Concepts and Technology*. New York, 1982.

UNTRACHT, O. 'The body encrusted: traditional jewellery from India', in *American Craft Magazine* vol. 40, no. 4, 1980.

UNTRACHT, O. *Jewelry Concepts and Technology*. New York, 1982.

VERNON-JACKSON, H. 'Craft workers in Bida', *Africa*, vol. 30, 1960.

VOGELSANGER, C. AND ISSLER, K. *Schmuck – Eine Sprache?* Zurich, 1977.

WAITE, D. *Artefacts from the Solomon Islands in the Julius L. Brenchley Collection*. London, 1987.

WANG-GO, W. AND YANG, B. *The Palace Museum Peking: Treasures of the Forbidden City*. London, 1982.

WANNYN, R. L. *L'Art Ancien du metail au Bas-Congo*. Brussels, 1961.

WARD, F. 'Jade stone of Heaven', in *National Geographic* 172:3, September 1987, pp. 282–315.

WATT, G. 'Indian art at Delhi, 1903', in *Delhi Art Exhibition, 1902–3*. Calcutta, 1903.

WEIR, S. *The Bedouin – aspects of the material culture of the Bedouin of Jordan*. London, 1976.

WILLEY, G. *An Introduction to American Archaeology* I. Chicago, 1966.

WILSON, V. *Chinese Dress*. London, 1986.

WOODLAND INDIAN CULTURAL EDUCATIONAL CENTRE. *Native Jewelry*. n.d.

WULFF, H. E. *The Traditional Crafts of Persia*. Cambridge Mass./London, 1966.

YAMANAKA, N. *The Book of Kimono*. Tokyo, 1982.

ZWALF, W. *Heritage of Tibet*. London, 1981.

Sources of the illustrations

Except for nos 3, 33, 103, 105, 106 and 156, which were photographed by Lee Boltin, all photos of objects in the British Museum were provided by the Museum's Photographic Service. The work of Ivor Kerslake, David Agar and Kate Waren in the Department of Ethnography is particularly appreciated. The maps were drawn by Noelle Derrett.

1 Angela Fisher
2 BM ETH 1947.Af8.2
3 BM ETH 1915–61
4 BM ETH 1975.As3.31
5 BM ETH 1900.5–24.34
6 Nigel Barley
7 BM ETH 86.11–29.83a
8 BM ETH 1987.Af3.1
9 P. N. Mago
10 Claus D. Brauns/Camera Press London
11 Robin Hanbury-Tenison/Camera Press London
12 Angela Fisher
13 M. O'Hanlon
14 BM ETH 1913.10–13.25 (top); 1954. Af23.1175
15 BM ETH 1904–161
16 BM ETH 1979.Af1.2950
17 BM ETH 1907.5–21.39
18 BM ETH 1928.7–12.5 (wood); 1949.Af46.651 (ivory)
19 BM ETH 1910.5–13.2–3
20 BM ETH 1933.11–14.82
21 Angela Fisher
22 BM ETH 1972.Af39.6c
23 BM ETH 1900.6–20.6a
24 BM ETH 1923.12–3.3
25 BM ETH 1947.Af13.679
26 BM ETH Q74.Af2914 (left), Q74.Af2919 (right)
27 BM ETH 1907.3–16.3
28 BM ETH 1936.10–5.12
29 BM ETH 1972.Af39.62
30 BM ETH (top, l. to r.) 1922.11–7.26; 1969.Af12.5; 1937.2–20.3; 1969.Af12.4; 1947.Af7.58; (bottom) 3173
31 Angela Fisher
32 BM ETH 1933.6–9.3
33 BM ETH 1942.Af4.1
34 Shelagh Weir
35 BM ETH 1956.As7.26a&b
36 BM ETH 1883.C0132.12a&b (ear-rings); 1883.C0132.12 (amulet-case), Henry Lansdell collection
37 Turkish and Islamic Art Museum, Istanbul: 482 (photo Reha Güney)
38 Topkapi Saray Museum, Istanbul: 2/2912 (photo Reha Güney)
39 Horniman Museum and Library, London 1981.512 (pendant), 1981.502 (buckle)
40 Jennifer Scarce (photo Ken Smith)
41 Jennifer Scarce (photo Ken Smith)
42 Philip Wilson Publishers
43 BM ETH 1973.As9.1,2 (amulet cases), 3 (pendant), 4 (belt)
44 BM ETH (l. to r.) 1975.As.3.48a,44a, 1988.As.6.8
45 Shelagh Weir
46 BM ETH 1959.As4.2 (top), 3 (bottom)
47 Longman Group UK Ltd
48 Longman Group UK Ltd
49 Jennifer Scarce
50 Oppi Untracht
51 Photo Verrier Elwin

52 Oppi Untracht
53 Oppi Untracht
54 Photo Sotheby's, New York
55 Photo Doranne Jacobson
56 Photo Sotheby's, London
57 Oppi Untracht
58 Oppi Untracht
59 Oppi Untracht
60 Collection Jean-Pierre & Colette Ghysels; photo Bruno Piazza
61 Oppi Untracht
62 Oppi Untracht
63 BM OA 2400, 2395, 2397
64 Oppi Untracht
65 Oppi Untracht
66 Sotheby's, New York
67 Oppi Untracht
68 Oppi Untracht
69 Collection Claire Untracht; photo Bobby Hanson
70 Oppi Untracht
71 Oppi Untracht
72 BM OA +14178
73 Oppi Untracht
74 Paul Lewis (courtesy of Hansjorg Mayer)
75 BM OA 1905.5–18.77
76 Horniman Museum and Library 24.10.53
77 BM OA 1893.2–5.117(40)
78 BM ETH 1959.As.10.7
79 BM OA 1981.11–13.1(1–5) (37)
80 BM OA 1905.5–31.1
81 Dr M. Parnwell, Centre for South-East Asian Studies, University of Hull
82 Hansjorg Mayer
83 Horniman Museum and Library 64.4.59/33–38
84 K. F. Wong, Sarawak (courtesy of The Oriental Museum, University of Durham)
85 BM OA (top to bottom, l. to r.) 2441, 2451, 2452, 2430, 2450
86 Horniman Museum and Library: de Zeote collection
87 Horniman Museum and Library 9115
88 BM ETH 1914.4–14.47 (neck ornament), 48–9 (ear ornaments)
89 BM ETH 1958.As.6.27a&b (pendants), 33 (neck-ring), 36 (necklace)
90 BM OA (top, l. to r.) CIG 114, 145; (bottom, l. to r.) + 340, CIG 132
91 BM OA 1981.8–8.11,8 (combs); 1974.5–13.20,21 (red and black lacquer/ivory pins); private coll.
92 BM ETH 1929.7–13.21
93 BM ETH 6398
94 Saffron Walden Museum, Beddoes collection 1925.28A
95 Marilyn Strathern
96 BM ETH + 3429 (left), + 3422 (right)
97 BM ETH 1931.7–14.33
98 Ulster Museum, Belfast, 1910.309A, 1910.309B
99 BM ETH Oc.25(32)
100 Saffron Walden Museum, Bernet collection 1835.373
101 Saffron Walden Museum, Ticknell collection 1836.82
102 BM ETH TAH 78
103 BM ETH TAH 57
104 BM ETH 1854.12–29.12, 1944.Oc.2.829
105 BM ETH 1854.12–23.11
106 BM ETH HAW 157, 156
107 BM ETH HAW 151
108 © Australian Institute for Aboriginal Studies

109 Ipswich Museum, Clement collection
110 Fitzwilliam Museum, Cambridge 0.51–1962
111 BM ETH 1929.7–12.1
112 Museo National de Costa Rica: 1.5(34); photo Dirk Dakker
113 Museum of the American Indian, Heye Foundation, New York; 16/1972B
114 BM ETH 1913.10–20.1
115 American Museum of Natural History, New York: V/C 1296
116 © Justin Kerr 1985, Instituto Hondureno de Antropologia y Historia, Tegucigalpa, Honduras
117 BM ETH +1669
118 The Metropolitan Museum of Art, New York; gift of H. L. Bache Foundation, 1969: 69.7.10
119 The Metropolitan Museum of Art, New York: 1979.206.733
120 American Museum of Natural History, New York (Landmann-Bird coll)
121 BM ETH + 5802
122 BM ETH Maudslay collection
123 BM ETH 1938.10–21.25
124 Anthony Shelton (photo British Museum)
125 BM ETH 1987.Am16.8
126 BM ETH 1952.Am12.15
127 BM ETH 1944.Am2.392
128 BM ETH 1972.Am7.30,31
129 Pitt Rivers Museum, University of Oxford
130 BM ETH Q72.Am.108
131 BM ETH +6992
132 BM ETH 1944.Am2.257
133 BM ETH 1903.50
134 BM ETH Van 211b–d
135 BM ETH Q79.Am7.6
136 BM ETH 1938.3–11.1
137 BM ETH 1925.5–8.4
138 BM ETH (left) 1959.Am.7.3; (right, top to bottom) 8204, 6832–3, 6834
139 University of Exeter Library
140 BM ETH 2004
141 BM ETH 1921.10–4.187–9
142 University of Exeter Library
143 BM ETH 1971.Am11.4–6
144 BM ETH 1973.As9.18
145 Oppi Untracht
146 BM ETH 1979.Am15.1a
147 Museo del Oro, Bogotá
148 Oppi Untracht
149 BM ETH (top to bottom) 1904.11–1.2; 1910.10–5.20; 1929.7–15.43; 1947.Af7.47; 1964.Af5.6; 1947.Af7.49
150 BM ETH 1920.7–5.26
151 BM ETH 1903.5–18.9
152 BM ETH 1970.As19.9
153 BM OA 1949.10–8.028
154 Collection Bandana Sen; photo Madan Mehta
155 Collection Anschel; photo A. C. Copper Ltd
156 BM ETH 1900.4–27.28
157 BM ETH +344–5
158 Photo Matti Salmi
159 Collection Jacques Carcanagues; photo Alan Fairley
160 Oppi Untracht
161 BM ETH 18–23
162 BM ETH 1971.As6.20 (pair), 31 (centre)
163 BM ETH 1938.7–6.1
164 BM OA 1938.5–24.252
165 BM ETH 1971.Af39.9
166 Victoria & Albert Museum, London 03408 (15)

Glossary and index